SPARKS
of the
DIVINE

SPARKS
of the
DIVINE

Finding Inspiration in Our Everyday World

Drew Leder

SORIN BOOKS NOTRE DAME, INDIANA

www.avemariapress.com

International Standard Book Number: 1-893732-81-9

Cover and text design by Brian C. Conley

Interior photographs © Beth Kingsley Hawkins www.hummerlady.com

Printed and bound in the United States of America.
Library of Congress Cataloging-in-Publication Data
Leder, Drew.
   Sparks of the divine: finding inspiration in our everyday world / Drew Leder.
   p. cm.
ISBN 1-893732-81-9 (pbk.)
 1. Spiritual life. I. Title.
BL624.L452 2004
204'.4--dc22

                                2004008606

For my wife, Janice McLane
and my daughters,
Anna-Rose and Sarah—
you are my sparks of the divine

Contents

Section One
The Natural World

Section Two
Object Lessons

Section Three
Human Being

Section Four
The Universe, Our Home

introduction

Spark-Hunting

When surgeons first became adept at cataract operations, they were able to restore sight to dozens who had been blind since birth. Many of the newly sighted were astounded by what they saw. Marius von Senden presented their cases in a book, *Space and Sight*, which in turn had a powerful effect on writer Annie Dillard, who quotes from it in *Pilgrim at Tinker Creek*.

One patient, after her bandages were unwrapped, describes a human hand—its function still unrecognized—as "something bright and then holes." Another was amazed to discover that each of her visitors had a totally different face. Who knew? A little girl stands speechless in a garden, then takes hold of "the tree with the lights in it," as she calls it. For many, the experience is arduous. A twenty-two-year-old woman was so overcome by her surroundings that she shut her eyes again for two weeks. Upon reopening them, "the more she now directed her gaze upon everything about her, the more it could be seen how an expression of gratification and astonishment overspread her features; she repeatedly exclaimed: 'Oh God! How beautiful!'"

Oh God, how beautiful! Oh God, now I *see*. Have we not had such experiences, albeit fleeting and maddeningly intermittent, of scales falling from our eyes and the world perceived anew?

The sheer ordinariness of things is our cataract. We view our day through a glaze of familiar tasks and objects. Ah yes, another

Wednesday. Ah yes, another tree by the side of the road, the ten thousandth we have seen and therefore no longer see at all. We glance at our to-do list and will never find written there—*encounter mystery; be dazzled and amazed; receive a great teaching from an unexpected source*. No, we're happy just to get the laundry done.

But there have been moments—we cannot deny them—when our world lit up as from a fire within. Perhaps it was the day we first fell in love; or went walking in a majestic forest; or found the solution that had so long eluded us to a problem which had plagued our life. Maybe it was that time we took off on a vacation, and the very expectation of novelty served as windshield wipers for the soul. Suddenly we are able to see afresh. We realize the beauty that surrounds us. Hidden at the heart of things we find lessons and reconciliations. A holy spirit, we sense, pervades the world—*this world*, even with its Wednesdays.

Kabbalah, the mystical branch of Judaism, tells a creation story that speaks to this spirit. When God made the world, wrote Isaac Luria in the sixteenth century, the divine light he emanated was so intense that it shattered the vessels containing it. The light fragmented into divine sparks (*nitzotzot*) which fell to earth. "Every particle in our physical universe, every structure and every being, is a shell that contains sparks of holiness," writes Rabbi David Cooper. But these sparks remain hidden in our ordinary world. Our sacred task as human beings is to uncover them, an act of cosmic restoration (*tikkun*). This we do through acts of service, prayer, loving kindness, and appreciation, whereby we attune to and celebrate the universe. We are here to heal the world by finding sparks of the divine, and in so doing to ourselves be healed.

This is no easy matter. Most self-help books tell us to seek healing through an inward journey. Examine and transform the contents of your mind. But can we use the mind, with its endless chatter and neuroses, as our primary tool to fix itself? This book advocates instead "going out of your mind"—finding healing in the lessons and blessings that surround us, the sparks that permeate the world.

To this end, the book is composed of one hundred brief reflections. Each seeks to discover a spark of the divine in everyday objects, activities, and experiences, and the glories of the natural world. Driving a car. Shaving. Cleaning out a filthy room. The ever-changing weather. The comic gravity of a frog. The spareness of a desert landscape. The delighted mess-making of a child confined in a high-chair. They will all become our teachers. We don't need to go to Tibet to find a sacred space and saintly guru. The teachings we need are right here and now if we but know how to *see*.

Accompanying each of the book's one hundred entries is a brief question or exercise meant to extend and personalize its meaning. They invite you to take the principle just discussed and play with applying it to your life. From a small spark a mighty fire can grow if you choose to fan the flames.

To further the book's use as a transformative tool, I also include fifteen guided meditations that take off from particular entries. I call these shape-shifts, for they are meant to assist you in shifting—bodily, mentally, spiritually—into the heart of another being. Here children may be our best teachers. A young girl pretends she is a flower opening her petals to the sun. The next moment she has transformed into a dog fetching a stick for her master. Through such shape-shifts, children master new styles of movement and awareness, play with a fluid sense of identity, and express empathy for the beings that surround them.

From where did that empathy first arise? Those who believe in reincarnation might say we feel for other creatures because once we *were* them: The memory is sedimented deep in our soul. From an evolutionary point of view, we are genetically related to all life and bred to fit—like a hand in a glove—to natural environments of forest, desert, and mountain.

Much of our physical and mental disease might be attributed to our loss of such relationships. We are cut off by our engineered environments, and the machine-like demands we place on ourselves, from a flowing communion with the more-than-human world. As a result, we tend to lose our humanity. We grow tense and tired without fully knowing why.

Chinese medicine emphasizes attunement to the four seasons of the changing year. Indigenous tribes are guided by a totem animal, such as an eagle or bear, with its unique powers. In Indian hatha yoga, when the body takes on the Cobra pose, or the Boat, or the Mountain, it accesses the flexibility, strength, and modes of awareness associated with these beings.

This is the intent of the "shape-shift" meditations I intersperse throughout the book, as well as many of the book's briefer questions and exercises. They invite you to step out of your habitual skin and mind, and enter into other forms.

Accompanying the essays are also sparks of inspiration, quotes garnered from many of the world's religions and the pens of artists and poets. The notion that the world is filled with holy sparks is hardly limited to Kabbalah. It is experienced by mystics across the planet and recorded in their sacred traditions. "The world is charged with the grandeur of God," writes Jesuit priest-poet, Gerard Manley Hopkins. "It will flame out like shining from shook foil." For Zen Buddhists, enlightenment comes the moment we realize that *samsara* (the created world) is none other than *nirvana* in disguise.

To get us started, here are some quotes from diverse religions. Notice how each uses its own conceptual language to articulate the sacred nature of the world. Notice as well the commonality of feeling that leaps beyond religious differences.

Christianity

Our time on earth should not be spent trying to transcend "worldly" things or the material world, but finding God in the midst of them. Jesus never denied the world. He went about instead discovering His Father everywhere in it. He saw spiritual significance in common things and actions: a lily, a grain of wheat, a mustard seed, bread, wine, water, doors, mending, sweeping, sewing. For Him, all was prayer and presence.

SUE MONK KIDD,
CONTEMPORARY AUTHOR,
GOD'S JOYFUL SURPRISE

Hinduism

All that [the *jnani-bhakti* seer-saint] sees he regards as forms of God. . . . In the majestic ocean he sees the grandeur of the Lord, in Mother Cow he sees the mother-like tenderness of God, in the earth he sees His patience, in the clear sky His purity, in sun, moon and stars, His brightness and beauty. . . . Thus he practices the art of seeing the one God at play everywhere, and doing so, one day, the seer-saint merges into the Lord.

ACHARYA VINOBA BHAVE,
TWENTIETH CENTURY TEACHER, *TALKS ON THE GITA*

Judaism

There is no sphere of existence, including organic and inorganic nature, that is not full of holy sparks which are mixed in with the *kelippot* (husks) and need to be separated from them, and lifted up.

ISAAC LURIA,
SIXTEENTH CENTURY TEACHER OF KABBALAH

Islam

Every branch, leaf and fruit
Reveals an aspect of His perfection
The cypress hints of His majesty,
The rose gives tidings of His beauty.

JAMI,
FIFTEENTH CENTURY PERSIAN POET

Goddess Worship

In the Craft, we do not believe in the Goddess—we connect with Her; through the moon, the stars, the ocean, the earth, through trees, animals, through other human beings, through ourselves. She is here. She is within us all.

STARHAWK,
CONTEMPORARY AUTHOR, *THE SPIRAL DANCE: A REBIRTH OF THE ANCIENT RELIGION OF THE GREAT GODDESS*

Native American

The mountains, I become part of it . . .
The herbs, the fir tree, I become part of it.
The morning mists, the clouds, the gathering waters,
I become part of it.

NAVAJO CHANT

Buddhism

People often ask me how Buddhists answer the question: "Does God exist?" The other day I was walking along the river. . . . I was suddenly aware of the sun, shining through the bare trees. Its warmth, its brightness, and all this completely free, completely gratuitous. Simply there for us to enjoy. And without my knowing it, completely spontaneously, my two hands came together, and I realized that I was making *gassho*. And it occurred to me that this is all that matters: that we can bow, take a deep bow.

EIDO SHIMANO ROSHI,
CONTEMPORARY ZEN ABBOT

Taoism

Do you want to work upon the world and improve it?
It won't work.
The world is sacred.
It can't be improved.
If you try to fix it, you'll ruin it.

TAO TE CHING, #29

Many religions, including ones cited above, have a world-denying strand. This world, we are told, is permeated by suffering, darkness, and illusion. Loosen our ties of attachment, we are warned. Withdraw from our sensuality, and the binding power of desire, that we may transcend and be free.

Yet the quotes above and throughout this book focus on another, complementary religious theme; that the world, rightly seen, is God's abode. Encounter it with humility, mindfulness, and reverence and you will be astonished by what you find. The most ordinary of things can radiate lessons and beauties. The very distinction between the secular and sacred dissolves.

In the prototypical mystical experience this can occur in a single blinding flash. The light of God suddenly and everywhere shines forth. This book presents a more patient, even piecemeal approach, for that may be more possible for many of us. (It is for me.) I call it the path of the *"slow-motion mystic."* This involves the bit-by-bit uncovering of holy sparks, now and then, here and there, as we are blessed to find them by the roadside. While any single experience may seem small, their cumulative effect is not. In slow-motion, we make genuine progress on the path to mystical awareness.

So journey through these one hundred insights, and use them to trigger a joy and attentiveness in the larger journey known as your life. There are many possible ways to travel through this book. In my own rush-rush life (full-time teaching, two young children) I may often have but a few minutes to read in bed, bathroom, or between household tasks. But I'd like in that time to be moved, enlightened, and inspired. Impossible? Not necessarily— Japanese haiku compress great meaning into seventeen syllables. My intent is similar, and so each essay is as brief as possible, taking but a few minutes to read. They are appropriate for morning or evening meditation, or a "spiritual snack" while on the run. Those with particular personal meaning may be worth lingering over and returning to, along with their associated questions or shape shifts.

The larger arc of the book organizes our spark-hunting by regions of the world. The first section explores sparks scattered throughout the natural world; its weather, creatures, elements, and landscapes. Section Two focuses on "object lessons" from the constructed world, as we invite the things we've made—cars, fire hydrants, beds, money—to become not just our servants but our teachers. Section Three focuses on "human *being*": what does it mean to *be human*, and do it well, and find holy sparks within our own body, our senses, mind, and emotions, even our sports and play? Section Four closes the book by returning to the broadest possible context—the entirety of the universe, and the "heavenly physics" whereby scientists now understand it. As a young child I would gaze at stars strewn across the vast distances and feel myself grow vacant, and wondering, and spacious, an experience both scientific and religious. But why even draw that distinction? The creation story given us by twenty-first century physics is as mystical and inspiring as any found in a holy text.

Though the ordering of essays has its logic, feel free to construct your own or to operate by chance and intuition. One of the fun features of spark-hunting is the serendipitous play of the unexpected. So you may wish to open the book at random, trusting to synchronicity that what your eye alights on will be just the thing. Or you might turn first to that book section or essay that particularly appeals. Perhaps you're intrigued by the notion of car-as-spiritual-teacher, and will leave the nature stuff for later.

You may also wish to hunt up pieces, spread throughout various sections, that address particular life issues you now face. In such a way, the book can be used as a self-help guide for personal transformation and healing. To aid this approach, at the end of this introduction I supply a sort of alternate table of contents that signals essays linked by underlying themes. For example, entries on "pits and seeds," "the desert," and "recycling garbage" are grouped under the theme of "Dealing With Dark Times." If you are dwelling in such darkness (and who among us, at times, isn't?) you might turn first to these entries in your search for sparks of light.

Whatever route is taken, the ultimate goal of the book is to render itself superfluous. You are learning how to take over the task of discovering divine sparks. The inspirations in this book are inevitably limited and channeled by my own sensibility. (For example, being a city dweller I have but a few entries based on wild animals; as a sports-lover, football and baseball are represented.) Your circumstances and enthusiasms undoubtedly differ from mine, and so shall your spark-hunting. Some of the experiences recorded in this book that deeply moved me may leave you cold. The solution: let them inspire you to find your own sparks.

To assist this, I close the book with some tips and suggestions for avid spark-hunters. You can even start reading there if you want, and then "play along" throughout the book, journaling about your own experiences even as you read some of mine. For it is not just this book you are exploring but the great Book of Creation, written in its language of wondrous creatures and landscapes, daily chores and duties, lovers and relatives, furniture and appliances, earth and sky, and on and on, amen.

Themes From the Book
(To help you locate selections that address particular life issues)

ONE

The Natural World

The Weather of the Soul

I think over again my small adventures,
My fears,
Those small ones that seemed so big.
For all the vital things
I had to get and to reach;
And yet there is only one great thing,
The only thing,
To live to see the great day that dawns
And the light that fills the world.

INUIT SONG

Every day is a god, each day is a god,
and holiness holds forth in time.

ANNIE DILLARD, HOLY THE FIRM

Dawn

HALLOWING THE BEGINNING

*G*o for an early morning walk—I mean *early*, before the sun has risen—to witness one of nature's great secrets: the dawn. Why call this a secret? Everyone knows that every day begins with sunrise, but things can be hidden by their familiarity. Just as a fish is unaware of the water in which it swims, and we take for granted so much of what we have (our health, our family, the food we eat), so we are likely to overlook the dawn. The sacred is a secret not because it is concealed, but because it is everywhere revealed, but not as *revelation*. "Only that day dawns to which we are awake," writes Thoreau. Yet how much we sleepwalk through life!

So let us awake to the dawn as revelation. The miracle of creation—"Then God said, 'Let there be light'; and there was light"—is reenacted each morning. To witness this is a privilege, like being present for the birthing of a child or the penning of a great symphony. What greater recreation than to witness *re-creation*, the world again leaping to life?

When we arise later we're likely to overlook the morning. After all, it's laid out like a lavish breakfast already there when we awaken. (Who then thinks much of the preparatory work that went into it?) We're apt to launch into the day far too quickly by virtue of greeting it too late. It's light out. Time to get going— dressed, fed, and off to work. But in hastily doing so we *profane* the day. From the Latin *"pro"* (before) and *"fanum"* (temple), to be profane is to be outside the temple, or as the dictionary says, "not initiated into the inner mysteries, not hallowed or consecrated." The day was not hallowed because it was not properly hello-ed. We wolf down our cereal and scan the morning paper with its usual morbid headlines. Yep, all is just as it was—only a little worse.

It need not be so. "Dawn" is an anagram for "wand." Let's reclaim the sense of dawn as a magic wand that waves the world alive. We need not be today as we were yesterday. Who knows what the magician will pull out of today's hat. A rabbit? A string of multi-colored scarves (not unlike the dawn itself)? All possibilities lie open, re-created afresh. This is the secret of the dawn, the sacred beginning of our day.

If you are used to waking early, tomorrow look out the window, or better, venture outside, and worship a bit at the feet of the dawn. If you're a late riser, consider getting up earlier one time this week to witness the day being born.

Wind

Opening to New Life

*L*ook out the window on a windy day. What do you see? Everything and nothing. The wind is everywhere, tumbling bits of newspaper end over end, pulling at hats clutched tightly to heads, snapping flags into salute. Yet the wind is also nowhere to be seen, invisible. No wonder God is imaged as speaking from a whirlwind. The wind, like the Divine, is everywhere and nowhere, ephemeral yet all-powerful, felt to the core of one's being, yet not to be contained and objectified.

No wonder, too, that the soul is imaged as wind. The Greek words for soul, *pneuma* and *psyche*, as the Hebrew *ruach*, as the Latin *spiritus*, all originally meant "breath." And the breath is a kind of life-sustaining wind. Meditate on the breath, counsel Buddhists— it is all there, the secret of life, the constancy of change, the *exchange* that each moment dissolves the borders that separate inner self from outer world. A wind blows through and connects us to all life. When it is blocked or departs we are dead.

No wonder, again, we feel kinship with the wind. True, in bitter cold we huddle against its violence. We are like a candle whose fragile fire might be extinguished. But more often a good wind whips up our spirit. We dance along with the dance that everywhere surrounds us—trees swaying excitedly, leaves snapping their castanets, the river shimmering with silvery ripples. In our staid house even the window blinds get rhythm, blown by the passing gusts.

Provided we have left the windows open. We can close them and turn the wind away, but this is like closing off the breath. Without new air, what will blow off the must and keep the house alive?

So, too, with ourselves. Shall we close our window to the Divine, that windy, breathing thing? "The spirit blows where it will. . . . you do not know where it comes from, or where it goes" (John 3:8). God cannot be captured in synagogue, church, or mosque, like some butterfly pinned in an album. No, Spirit blows through in the form of wind. It rattles our blinds, puffs away the dust, and rearranges our plans.

Is there an area of your life in which you have shut the window and let things grow musty?

Consider opening the window wide, or at least a crack, through prayer or reflection on what might be done differently.

Praised be you, my Lord with all your creatures, especially Sir Brother Sun, Who is the day and through whom You give us light. And he is beautiful and radiant with great splendor, and bears a likeness of You, most High One.

ST. FRANCIS OF ASSISI,
"THE CANTICLE OF BROTHER SUN"

The Sun

Mother-Father of Us All

Where does the sun begin or end? Does it terminate at the perimeter of the yellow disk I see traveling through the sky? But I only see it when its light hurtles across ninety-three million miles into my eyeballs. The sun is not just "up there" but inside me, rattling about my nervous system.

It is also in the tree, providing energy for each new leaf to sprout and capture more sun. It is there in the bird who eats the worm who feasts on that tree-leaf. Thus the sun is in that bird's song, and my ear that hears it, and my whole body fueled on sun-fed wheat.

We are all sun-worshipers. The flower lifts up its petals in prayer. The tree grows ever higher, longing for the Lover. The baby awakens in the crib, pleased to greet the morning. We are a sun-drenched planet—trees, birds, worms, flowers, babies—all sucking at the great solar teat.

No wonder cultures the world over have prayed to sun-gods, *Ra* of the Egyptians, the Hindu *Surya*, and so many others. For Plato, the best metaphor for the Form of the Good, source of Being and Knowledge, was the sun. By its light we are both nourished (given being), and en-lightened (given the ability to know).

Should we let a day go by without thanks? "Dear Sun, heavenly Father-Mother, we gather at your feet. We thank you for the gift of life you spill so generously from the heavens. Sacred star, our blood is made of your photons. And so we on earth are all one blood with each other, black and white, male and female, human, tree, and worm."

Yet, we do not always bear witness to the sun. It disappears throughout the long night. It hides behind clouds, or we ourselves hide from it by going inside, shielding our face, or closing our eyes. Amazing, that we can block off a celestial orb nearly a million miles in diameter using an eyelid less than an inch across. Amazing, but adaptive. Without a shield, our retinas, overwhelmed by light and power, could be burned blind.

Maybe the same is true of our relationship to the Divine. Though the world is fed on this Light and Power, it is often absent from view. Even saints experience a "dark night of the soul" where God is nowhere to be found. Then, too, most of us focus on our petty ends which, small as a hand held over the eyes, can yet block out the Cosmic Source. To a degree this oblivion is necessary to ordinary life. It is said that no one can look directly at the face of God and live (Judges 13:22). The egoic "I" is destroyed by mystic illumination, as the eye is by staring at the sun.

But whether obscured by night, cloud, haze, or eyes shut tight, the Light is ever present. It birthed us. It watches over us. It feeds us in countless ways. It is within us, in our breath and our blood. We inhabitants of earth are all sparks of the Divine, and sparks of the nurturing sun.

When eating a meal today, pause to think how this food is all sunlight transformed. Remind yourself you are a being made of light, eating light to renew yourself. And if you go for a walk try to see around you the sun at the heart of all things—the grass, the trees, the houses, the people who built them. . . .

SHAPE-SHIFT:
Pretend You Are the Rising Sun

BENEFITS: enhanced energy; sense of connection to the universe

Find a comfortable seated position; for example, sitting cross-legged on a cushion or firmly centered on a chair. After taking a few moments to breathe deeply and relax, visualize the sun as if located in your abdomen a little below the navel. Imagine this is an early morning sun, perhaps surrounded by the delicate colors of the dawn. Breathe into your abdomen, as if the in-breath fuels this sun, helping it to glow.

After a couple of minutes allow this sun to rise to the center of your chest. Now breathe into this heart-region. The sun is strengthening as it rises. Feel its golden warm rays spread through your torso, out to your limbs, and up to your head. Also, feel these rays emanating outward from your heart-sun. If you wish, send some of this love-energy to a specific person in need.

After a couple of minutes, allow the sun to rise yet again, through your neck and out the top of your head so it rests just above you like a golden crown. Send your breath upward to this region. Feel the sun's rays shooting outward, lighting up the universe and all beings within it. Enjoy this sensation of spreading beyond the self. Enjoy being the sun.

This meditation, which uses Hindu *chakras* or energy centers, is a good way to get started in the morning.

Cloudy Days

Heavenly Comforter

*F*unny, that a cloudy day can provide so much food for the soul. It is the sun that feeds all living creatures, directly or indirectly, with energy. And there's no denying that a sunny day can be cheering: Golden sustenance shines down from the heavens. But there is something just as rich about a cloudy day, and not only the ones when wind-blown clouds alternately conceal and reveal the sun like some fan-dancer titillating the customer. Here I celebrate the truly overcast day with nary a ray to be seen.

For clouds create a calm mood. Life's sharp shadows are erased. There's no need to don dark glasses to save your eyes from a solar assault. The nimbus and cumulus protect you. The world is at rest, cuddled down beneath a comforter flung across the sky.

Clouds give us permission to be where we are: a little depressed perhaps, or lazy, or introspective, or just plain quiet as we sip a cup of tea. When in such moods, a bright day can seem accusatory: get up, get going, get cheerful! The sun stares down like a yellow happy face, demanding response in kind. But a cloudy day protects and accepts us. If the sky can cloud over, so may we.

The psalmist writes that God "will hide me in his shelter in the day of trouble; he will conceal me under the cover of his tent" (Psalm 27). In this Middle Eastern desert, the tent provides a refuge from enemies, but also from the blazing sun. Clouds are such a tent, spread across the heavens, offering us Godly shelter.

Don't curse the next cloudy day that comes along. Instead, use its soft energies to relax a bit, to be quiet and do some inner-exploration or healing.

Rain

Discovering Our Vegetative Soul

*L*isten to the rain. On a good and rainy day (why do we reserve the term "good weather" for sunshine?) it drums on the world like fingertips on a table. Listen more closely, and it sounds almost like speech with subtle changes of pace, mood, and intensity.

But what does rain *say?* Listen even closer. Here is what I hear (you may hear more): "Calm down. There's nothing that *must* be done. There's nowhere you must go. So stop. Listen. Be still."

Or else, "Sadness is all right. Grieving is natural. Tears are okay. The earth, and your soul, are watered by rain. Without this the world would grow parched."

Or, "Listen to My heart's song. I will never forget you, I will never forsake you. I come toward you, ever toward you, in the rain. Just receive."

Aristotle said that human beings have tripartite souls. Through our "rational soul" we deliberate and choose. Beneath that lies an "animal soul." This is the part of our nature shared with other animals, whereby we perceive sense-objects and pursue them through locomotion. But even deeper than that lies a "vegetative soul." Like plants, we absorb and digest, grow and reproduce. We hold all levels of nature within.

From your point of view as a rational animal, rain is likely an annoyance. You can't get to your destination without water from the skies splashing on your head, obscuring your vision, creating mud and hazards. "Bad weather," the meteorologist intones, speaking from this restless plane.

But try experiencing rain from your vegetative soul. If you were a plant you could not wander to a cafe for a cooling drink. Anchored to earth, you are thirsty, vulnerable, dependent. You must wait upon the water that falls like manna from heaven. To a plant, rain comes as a life-saving grace, no matter how often it has previously occurred.

"Isn't the rain beautiful?" [Brother Elias, a hermit] said. *"Why do we keep resisting rain? Why do we only want the sun when we should be willing to be soaked by the rain? The Lord wants to soak us with his grace and love. Isn't it marvelous when we can feel the Lord, in so many ways and get to know him better and better!"*

HENRI J.M. NOUWEN,
THE GENESEE DIARY: REPORT
FROM A TRAPPIST MONASTERY

So to best appreciate rain you must rest in your plant-self: your vegetative soul. Quiet the chattering mind and the anxious body. Grow a little more still. Be silent. Listen. Then you'll feel the rain, like holy water from above, quenching your thirsty soul.

When next it rains, take a few minutes to appreciate it as if from your plant-soul. Be quiet. Drink it in. Receive its messages. Do you hear it saying anything to you?

Snow

Heaven on Earth

*W*hy is it that children so delight in a world freshly coated in snow? (And adults, too, if in touch with their child-mind.) We cannot *make it happen,* no matter how powerful our desire for a day off with free time for sledding. We must hope and wait, like a person in prayer, for magic to descend from the skies.

But when it comes, oh man, what a revelation! The world is created anew. Tree limbs are strung with diamond necklaces; a sidewalk turns into a highway of light; houses wear powdered wigs like eighteenth century noblemen. It is all different, like the world we awaken to when our heart has been touched by love.

This pure world of snow has not yet been sullied by the trails of our complex wanderings, the grime of urban life, the mud of truck tires, or our heedless refuse. For a time, at least, it lies white and silent. Snow covers over, *forgives* the sins of the world. Yes, we will sin again, we will trample on this grace. We always do. But for a moment we can imagine otherwise.

Children glide down a snowy hill as on angel's wings. Adults gather round the fireplace released from their cares. The frenetic grows calm; the disparate is united. From the slum to the mansion, all dons the same garment. We can dream for a time of a better world—no, we can *experience* it, for snow is heaven fallen to earth.

When next it snows, imagine this as a cleansing energy that heals and renews the world. Or instead (especially for those in warmer climes or seasons), you can visualize an inward snow that covers over what feels grimy or jagged inside. Let this image be a source of positive renewal for the day ahead.

Rainbows

The Messy Beauty of Emotions

Somewhere over the rainbow. . . ." What is it about a rainbow that unlocks our dreams? First, its spectacular palette, a blend of—well, all the colors of the rainbow, shimmering and luminescent. Then, too, the form of the artwork—a gentle arc that spans the sky kissing the earth on each end. "Thy will be done on earth as it is in heaven"—the rainbow suggests in physical form what such an intersection might look like. On the ceiling of the Sistine Chapel, Michelangelo painted God's finger stretching toward Adam's. So, too, the rainbow stretches its fingers between heaven and earth. At its end may lie a pot of gold, or even, a pot of God.

But think for a moment about the source of a rainbow. This vision of perfection is the product of messy opposition. It is not made of pure sunshine alone, nor of the earth-sustaining rain. You only get a rainbow when you have both at once, engaged in a playful quarrel.

Not a bad description of the human heart—as it is, not as we might wish. It would be nice to be happy all the time. Some spiritual movements preach the unremitting production of positive thoughts and joyful moods. Make, by force of will, every day sunny. Vanish clouds through mental control.

On the other extreme, we may fall prey to moods that render our world a constant dark. Depression settles in like a solid bank of clouds. Not a ray of sunshine peeps through.

A monotone world, whether sunny or overcast, will never produce a rainbow. But luckily, human beings are granted a full palette of colors: the pinks of optimism; the grays of the humdrum day; the delicate greens of new life and hope; the dark blue of heartfelt love; the reds of stormy passion. Why all this? Because the soul is not just meant for sunshine, or for rain. It contains both, refracting off of one another with varied and spectacular effects.

We may wish our emotional life were simpler, but this is not the way of heaven and earth. We are meant to experience the full rainbow of emotions. Out of messy, inconstant, self-contradictory weather is born a precious arc.

Today, simply observe some of your changing emotions with appreciation, as you might appreciate a rainbow. You don't have to stop sadness, or anger, or joy. Just view them as the different colors of the rainbow.

Thunderstorms

Shattering the Familiar World

*E*ver stood in the midst of a thunderstorm? The effect is (literally) electrifying. Jagged bolts of lightning suddenly illuminate the sky. A pregnant pause follows, an uncanny stillness—then the *boom* of thunder crashing over the rooftops, rattling the windows of small children. Sheets of rain pour down as if Noah's flood has come to wash away the world.

Hooray! For as frightening as a thunderstorm can be, it is also exhilarating. We are galvanized (from Galvani, the eighteenth century investigator of electricity) by its sheer power and drama. A sunny day grants energy. On an overcast day, clouds cuddle the world, providing puffy pillows. Spring chirps us gently awake with a bird trill. Autumn nestles us under its multicolored quilt. Every day and season has its subtle charms. Ah, but sometimes we need the thunderstorm like a bat out of hell, armed with terror and phosphorus, to mess things up. It is demonic, but also heavenly. At Mt. Sinai Yahweh speaks to Moses in thunder; Indra, chief deity of the Vedas, was the god of storms; Zeus, head of the Greek pantheon, was the thunder god. This is a natural power turned *supernatural*.

When the gods come thus we tend to run and hide. Scamper out of the rain. Pull down the windows. Muffle the noise. Crawl under the covers. Look for Julie Andrews to sing "My Favorite Things" as she does during a thunderstorm in *The Sound of Music:* "Raindrops on roses / And whiskers on kittens / Bright copper kettles / And warm woolen mittens. . . ." We thus struggle to restore the familiar.

But what if we did the opposite? What if we used every thunderstorm to change our lives?

A thunderstorm develops in conditions of instability. Columns of warm air rise, then condense when they meet the cool air of the higher atmosphere. The large cloud that forms develops regions of positively and negatively charged ions. Finally, the tension grows too great. It is discharged as a lightning bolt releasing pent-up energy.

Isn't our life often in need of something similar? Tensions develop within and without. Between our spiritual longings and our mundane pursuits. Between different aspects of our personality which cannot easily be reconciled. Between ourselves and our loved ones, ourselves and our culture. It's like the murky, humid air that precedes the thunderstorm, filled with irresolution.

Then suddenly, release! Boom! Crash! Sudden illumination. Flashes of inspiration. Pulsating action. Something's happening at last.

So when a thunderstorm occurs outside, throw open the window and let it in. Embrace the gods of the storm. Seize the moment to reorganize your life. Destroy what must go. Light up what is of value. Shout forth the truest needs of your heart.

For the world that follows the thunderstorm is peaceful and renewed. The oppressive heat has been cleared out, the soil rendered moist by the rainfall. The song of the birds is a little sharper, and everything smells refreshed. So, too, can our life be after the storm. Praise Yahweh, praise Indra, praise Zeus.

When next a thunderstorm comes, enjoy its transformative energies. Use it as a prayerful time to see what needs to be changed and released in your life. Or, you can initiate this sort of prayer and meditation by visualizing a thunderstorm within.

Creature Teachers: Plants and Animals

We call upon the forests, the great trees
reaching strongly to the sky with earth in their
roots and the heavens in their branches, the fir
and the pine and the cedar, and we ask them to:
Teach us and show us the way.
We call upon the creatures of the fields and
forest and the seas, our brothers and sisters the
wolves and deer, the eagle and the dove, the
great whales and the dolphin, the beautiful Orca
and salmon who share our Northwest home, and
we ask them to: Teach us and show us the way.

EXCERPT FROM A CHINOOK BLESSING LITANY

Trees

A Teacher for Life

A tree has much to teach us about how to live well. Let's start
with its root message, for from its roots the tree gains moisture, nutrients, and stability. If the tree is to grow to its full size it
needs an extensive root system. Otherwise it's vulnerable to toppling over in a storm. And so, too, for us. We need to be rooted in
whatever it is that truly feeds us—be it prayer, meditation, family,
nature, intimate relations, or healing solitude. Then and only then
may we spread branches and leaves (our complex engagements in
the world) without fear of toppling over in an exhausted frenzy.
Before increasing our involvement we had best deepen our roots.
This will keep us strong and balanced.

If a tree's roots support its branches and leaves, the reverse is
also true. Leaves gather energy from the sun that in turn is used
to feed the whole tree. So, too, should our leaves—our relationships and duties—be a place where we gather energy, not lose it.
One person joins the PTA. Another launches an ambitious project at work. A third restores a classic car with his daughter. A
fourth works two jobs to make ends meet. So many different
branches and leaves. Yet there is but one question to ask—will this
outgrowth harvest energy, or does it instead deplete resources? If
the latter, prune it away at once.

For a tree does not fear change. It teaches well the art of
transformation. In spring it puts out buds to catch the early sun.
When winds come it sways in harmonic motion, rather than stiffly
resisting. In the fall, it knows when best to change its garments.
Off comes the green coat of chlorophyll and on go the vestments
of yellow and red to better absorb the fading light. Finally, the tree
does not fight winter and its pronouncements of death but wisely
adapts. It sheds leaves, reducing itself to a skeleton until the time
of resurrection.

Would that we were that accepting of life's storms, and of the larger rhythms of the lifecycle. Would that we felt that deeply anchored in the earth, that nurtured by energy from the heavens.

But how to develop these capacities? We need not travel distant lands in search of a guide. Merely sit beneath the nearest tree. Lean against its trunk. Enjoy its shade. Listen deeply to its teachings. Here is guru enough for our needs.

Ask yourself, what practices keep you firmly rooted? Are you using them? Of your many branches and leaves (worldly involvements), are there any that need pruning? Are you flowing appropriately with the winds of change that blow through your life, or are you stiffly resisting? Use these questions to help you make your tree of life a little healthier.

Pretend You Are a Tree

BENEFITS: bodily and mental healing and balance

Sit down in a well-supported way on a chair or on the ground. Have your back straight but not rigid. Begin to imagine that instead of a human body you have the body of a tree. Take a few moments to feel the root structure that connects you deeply to the vital energies of the earth. Imagine a network of tree roots extending downward from your buttocks or your feet.

Then begin to turn your attention to the upper part of your body. Experience it as your branches and leaves. Imagine them receiving the energy of the sun and using it to feed your body. Feel your torso as if it were the tree's trunk, mingling energies from above and below.

Use your breath to deepen this meditation. With each inhalation focus on your upper body, your branches and leaves. Feel them breathing in the healing, growth-producing, and illuminating energy that comes from the sky. With each exhalation, send this energy down through your trunk, into your legs, and out through your root system into the earth.

Continue with this movement skyward, then earthward, on each complete breath. If you wish, you may silently say to yourself "Heaven" on the in-breath, and "Earth" on the out-breath. As a tree, you are both heavenly and grounded.

This meditation is indebted to the Chinese Qigong (Chi Kung) tradition, with its balancing of yang and yin, heaven and earth energies, through movement, breathing, and meditation.

Trees and Humans

A Sacred Marriage

*F*eel like making love to a tree? Like it or not (and I do) you're engaged in it right now. Because to breathe is to be in intercourse with trees, and really with plants of all sorts.

You may remember something like this from high school biology, but probably didn't consider it deeply (who does in high school biology?). Oxygen is discarded at the end of a tree's photosynthetic process. To create tree-flesh—bark and branch, leaves and fruit—the tree combines energy from the sun and carbon dioxide, and gives off oxygen as a by-product. We do something of the reverse—take the tree's oxygen and combine it with our food to make our carbon-based flesh, then exhale leftover carbon dioxide. The tree's out-breath is our in-breath, and vice-versa, in a ceaseless exchange of love.

Exchange yes, but why call this love? Because it is so closely akin to certain aspects of human love. Between tree and person there is interpenetration, body entering body. Each supports and nurtures the other. The one's well-being is inextricably tied to that of the partner. Boundaries between self and other fall away—the two are woven together in a way that creates a greater whole. As recited in a marriage ceremony, "A man will leave his father and his mother, and be united with his wife, and the two will become one flesh" (Genesis 2:24). We are bio-married to trees, breathing life into each other.

But as in any marriage, partners can become estranged. One may be more responsible than the other for this alienation of affection. Here it is clear who's at fault. Trees have never abandoned us no matter how we have clear-cut forests or poisoned them with acid rain. We are like the abusive spouse who thinks his harsh treatment justified, his power ultimate and therefore correct. But when power ruins love, both partners suffer. As tree-breath fails, so does our own, choked with pollutants and global warming.

Let us seek, then, to be more appreciative of our spouse. Each time we breathe in let us feel the tree's kiss entering our very body. As we breathe out, let us be aware of graciously returning the gift. Then we live in the present, and *live life as a present.*

And even death cannot part whom God hath joined together. A tree's death feeds the soil that in turn feeds us. In our death, we also return dust to dust. Gifting our carbon to the earth, we may exchange our human flesh for the bark of trees. Ours is truly a marriage made in heaven—but realized on the bountiful earth.

Next time you go for a walk, pause before a tree and feel the exchange of breath and life between the two of you. You may wish to offer thanks to the tree and/or to God.

Weeping Willows
Shelter in Time of Sorrow

Look carefully at a weeping willow and see how well it is named. The branches and leaves slope toward the ground like someone bent over and soft with tears. When we cry we often sag in this way. We are too weary to battle gravity, too humbled to assume a haughty posture. We are past the point of putting on a show of strength for our fellows. Tears are a release and a relaxation, a part of our body flowing down to Earth—the Mother from which we first emerged, and to whom we return in death.

Because the weeping willow assumes this posture, it forms a perfect shelter for those who would weep. Try it. You can sit beneath a tall pine and find little solace. But lean against the trunk of a weeping willow and you are surrounded by a hundred arms and hands, all soft, caressing, gently blown by the wind. Unlike Jesus' crown of thorns, you now wear a crown of green fingers which seem bent on massaging away your tension, wiping your tears, letting you know you are loved. The weeping willow understands your sorrow because it seems to have shared in it.

And we can be like weeping willows for one another. Seeking solace?—go to the man or woman who has also known tears, and been changed by their pain from pine to willow. And let yourself so be changed as it's needed. When life blows cruel it is tempting to fight back, yet the stiff branch cracks off in the wind. Instead, find your weeping willow nature and be soft, quiet, and tearful.

Then, guaranteed, will come a time when someone else will gather beneath the hanging branches you have formed. Your tears will not be wasted. One day, they will ease the pain of another who comes to you for respite. And this, in turn, will help that person become a weeping willow able to shelter someone else. In this way do we seed one another, even when that seed is tears.

Who (or what in nature) has served for you as a weeping willow, giving shelter in time of sorrow? Are you doing that for yourself, and for others in need?

❖

What is the test that you have indeed undergone this holy birth? Listen carefully. If this birth has truly taken place with you, then every single creature points you toward God.

MEISTER ECKHART,
MEDIEVAL CHRISTIAN MYSTIC

❖

Pits and Seeds

Failure as Growth

*W*e all have experiences of failure. Life is filled with them, the way a watermelon is filled with pits. Sometimes life seems the pits, more than the sweet. Why? Where is the grace, what is the point, of all this failure we suffer through?

It may help to remember that pits are really seeds. Okay, they're not so good to eat. They are hard, bitter, resistant. But that's because they're not meant to serve us, but to bring about the next watermelon. And that melon will also have seeds scattered throughout its flesh, to give rise to the next melon, and so on. Call it a melon-choly truth: You can't have the fruit without the seed. In fact, the seed is the fruit being born.

And so, too, with those things we call "failures." They may be the seeds, not yet ripe, of sweet things yet to come. True, they are bitter and hard. A lost job. A broken relationship. A vice disruptive to our well-being and to that of those around us. We feel keenly our failures in life. Yet they can be the seeds (if we nurture them properly) from which we grow—what? Humility. Compassion for our own weakness and that of others. Dependence upon a God who loves and accepts failures even when everyone else condemns.

We also grow new strengths of character and wisdom, new forms of courage and perseverance, new skills and abilities, as we struggle to accept, work with, or surmount the failures which inevitably seed our lives.

Face it: we're *supposed to fail*, just as a watermelon is supposed to have seeds. Otherwise, we might gorge on life's sweetness, but life's growth and generativity would stop. So when a failure occurs, try to see it as a seed. Don't just discard it. Plant it in the soil of your soul. If need be, water it with your tears. But also douse it in the sunshine of hope and faith that one day, perhaps soon, perhaps later, when the season is right, that seed will break open and sprout forth a plant, densely vined and laden with fruit.

Look at one or more areas where you have been experiencing "failure." Can you see ways in which these pits have or could be seeds for personal and spiritual growth?

❖

O Great Spirit, whose voice I hear in the winds and whose breath gives life to all the world, hear me.
I am small and weak. I need your strength and wisdom.
Let me walk in beauty and let my eyes ever behold the red and purple sunset.
Let me learn the lessons you have hidden in every leaf and rock.

EXCERPT FROM A PRAYER
SOMETIMES ATTRIBUTED TO THE SIOUX

❖

Soil

Caring for the Self

*S*oil—as a word it is so close to *soul*. And in many ways soil is soul-like. It includes within it a principle of life. It breathes this vital force into plants, as the soul is said to breathe life into the body. Then, too, the soil is connected to larger energies like sunlight and rain, just as the soul is fed by the Transcendent. The earth is alive because it is *ensoiled*, just as a person is ensouled.

But the soil can be depleted. If all we do is extract nutrients from it to grow our crops, soon it becomes exhausted and yields diminish. We might say the same of our souls. Each day the world and we, ourselves, tax our energies with fresh demands—produce this result, purchase that thing, fix this problem. Rich plants may grow from our soul-work; for example, we may be raising a child who is healthy and strong. But at the same time we risk depleting our own reserves. Ask any parent at the end of a long day.

If we, too, are to keep our vitality, we need the twin protectors of soil: rest and fertilizers. A farmer will let a field lay fallow when it needs to recover its strength. That farmer will also return nutrients to the soil through the use of appropriate fertilizers. Should we do any less for the soul?

So ask yourself, what are your fertilizers? Spending time alone, or carousing with your buddies? Relaxing into a novel, or taking a brisk country walk? Praying to the Source of goodness and light? Or gobbling down a double scoop of chocolate ice cream in front of the TV? Don't be quick to pronounce moral judgments on your preferences—sometimes the best fertilizer can be table scraps and dung.

Equally important is to let your field lie fallow. The world may accuse you of being (God forbid) *nonproductive*. Actually, this down-time may bear abundant fruit through a renewal of creative energies.

Too much toil is not good for soil—and it likewise takes its toll on the soul.

Are you fertilizing your soul and letting it lie fallow? If not, how might you better do so?

Flowers

Turning Toward the Light

*M*any flowers are "heliotropic." In less fancy language, that means they seek out the sun. They turn their faces upward, open petals in the morning, and follow the sun on its daily path. At night they close up shop until their sun-god next arises.

If flowers are heliotropic, we might call human beings theotropic. We turn our faces toward the heavens in search of the living God. Since "the kingdom of heaven is within you," this may mean seeking an Inward Light.

Of course, humans often turn from Spirit toward a thousand other goals. One person chases money. Another gets his thrill shooting up drugs. A third makes a god out of success and spends long hours at the office. A fourth takes off on a pleasure yacht with little thought for those left on shore. Man's inhumanity to man is legendary, as is our propensity to worship golden calves.

But what is a golden calf but a dim reflection of Spirit? Its gold is like a pale imitation of the sun's golden hue. The worldly value of gold is an earthly reminder of that which is of truest value—"the pearl of great price"—our connection to Spirit. Whether we shoot up drugs, stuff our face with food, chase after money, or lust for sex, aren't we seeking, after all, *fulfillment:* that which will somehow fill us full, as a flower is by sunlight? In a sense, aren't we still searching for God?

I said we were theotropic, I didn't say we were good at it. Put a flower in an artificially lit environment and you can disorder its heliotropic reactions. It will chase after fluorescent light but is unlikely to find the same nourishment there as in many-hued sunlight. After all, the flower was created by and for the sun.

So too for us. We have become enamored of the artificial lights we turn on such as material wealth, drugs, and power. We inhabit cities that are like fluorescent hothouses but we never feel fully fed.

So different is our relation to the sunlight of the Spirit. This is not a light we made ourselves, nor can command with a flick of the switch. All we can do is open our petals. Wait. Yearn. Follow where we are guided. Sometimes we seem to sit in darkness but let us be ever assured: The sun will rise, the day does come, and we shall be fed with Light.

What are the forms of "artificial light" that sometimes become the goals of your life? When are you more like the flower, opening to the true sun of Spirit?

Frogs

Speaking and Acting From a Deep Place

"*Ribbit!*" Let it rip! Children love to imitate a frog's cry. It emerges from a deep place in the gullet and is at once serious and joyful. Nothing superficial about that statement: The frog's whole being seems to condense in the sound. Yet until that moment the frog has long sat silent, conserving its energy.

The frog doesn't engage in idle chatter. He doesn't chirp on like certain birds who trill the whole day through. His silence is silence; his speech is speech. Much of the principle of "Right Speech," a part of the Buddha's Eightfold Path to enlightenment, has to do with what is *not* said: harsh words, lies, useless blabber. Engage in speech, the Buddha declared, only when it improves on silence. In our culture we are inundated by words—a single magazine might contain some fifty thousand—but how many meet that test? The frog's croak does. His is "right speech," resonant and full.

What the frog does with silence and sound it duplicates in movement and stillness. Whether on the banks of a stream, or poised on a lily pad, the frog impassively sits. It bides its time, waiting for a bug to approach, then—*whoosh*—tongue darts out and snatches the prey. No wonder the frog is celebrated in Zen painting and poetry. It is a symbol of the enlightened being who knows how to be still. How to await the proper moment, then seize an opportunity with decisive action. No wasted motion. No agonies of anticipation or regret. Just sit. Wait. Then act.

But how often we are anti-frogs. We rush about restlessly creating havoc, propelled by worries and a desire to control. We would rather be in the know than in the Now. As a result we live clumsily in an imagined future instead of gracing the present with our presence. As an anti-frog we are likely to miss the fly. The moment to act comes and departs, as we consider, reconsider, then regret.

Not so the frog. Its very cry cuts through all that nonsense: *"Ribbit!"* Yes, let us emulate this noble example. In fairy tales a maiden's kiss turns a yucky frog back to a prince. Maybe we've got it all wrong. Wouldn't it be better if the princes of our world could speak and act a bit more like frogs?

Pick a troublesome situation in your life. Ask yourself, are you being like a frog: waiting in stillness until the appropriate moment to speak or act decisively? If not, how might you apply this lesson?

Ducks

The Paddling Beneath the Glide

A duck (or a goose or swan) demonstrates two types of motion, one visible, one concealed. Above the water, all is smooth. The duck glides effortlessly forward, a picture of tranquility and repose. Beneath the surface things look different. The little webbed feet are furiously paddling, propelling the duck along.

Above, the glide; below, the paddle. This, at least for a good long time, describes the spiritual life. We may wish to make progress effortlessly, as if wafted along by a holy wind. Some spiritual or self-help books make it seem this easy. Simply adopt the right attitude, or trust your intuition, or rely on God, and all will be smooth sailing.

Often, the reality is more challenging. Without effort, we're more likely to sink than to glide. Beneath the surface there's a lot of work to be done if we wish to make palpable progress. We must honestly face where we've screwed up our life—and sometimes the lives of others—through our storms of selfishness, resentment, and fear. We must reveal such truths to sympathetic listeners, and if possible clean up our messes. We must apply our mind toward knowing our mind. We must seek spiritual help with inner transformation, whether through prayer, chanting, communal worship, or meditation. We must avoid overindulgence in our particular temptations. It matters not whether they are socially dubious, like drug addiction, or socially sanctioned, like money-hunger and careerism.

In short, there's a fair amount of paddling to be done. We need to exercise our little webbed feet. Much of this work can and should be invisible to others—done in the early morning or at night before retiring, or throughout the day hidden in the depths of our heart. Jesus said, "When you fast, put oil on your head and wash your face, so that your fasting may be seen not by others but by your Father who is in secret" (Matthew 6:17–18). Otherwise, our efforts may turn into self-congratulatory spiritual exhibitionism. Webbed feet do little good above the surface.

If all goes well (though progress is inevitably bumpy) people will mostly see the surface glide. "You're so even-tempered," they may say. "Nothing seems to faze you. I guess that's just the way you are." Little do they know that whatever glide we've achieved is the outcome not of ease but of effort.

That effort need not be an onerous burden. Ducks rarely look exhausted. The buoyancy of the water, the whisper of the breeze, the sheer joy of movement, refreshes. So, too, the movement of the spirit, which releases divine energies. Yet it doesn't happen without the paddling. The Holy Spirit in Christianity may be imaged as a dove, but it befriends the spiritual duck.

What kind of below-the-surface paddling have you found most helps you to glide successfully through life? Are you remembering to paddle in these ways?

Migrating Birds

That Most Wild and Necessary Journey

❖

All birds are messengers; they teach us to rise above the situation, to be free and rise above.

SARA SMITH,
MOHAWK TRIBE,
FROM *SIMPLY LIVING: THE SPIRIT OF INDIGENOUS PEOPLE*

❖

*I*n certain Hindu texts the sound of "*hamsa*" (pronounced "humsuh") is recommended as a mantra for meditation. In Sanskrit it means "I am That." The true self (*aham*) is one with That (*sa*), the divine ground of all things. I am much more than just the separate ego-self; I hold God and the universe within.

It is said that from birth we repeat *hamsa* with every breath. Listen closely: You may hear a slight "hu" sound on the in-breath, and a sigh ("sa") on the out-breath. We need not repeat this natural mantra so much as attune to it. The movement of air as we breathe also confirms "I am That." The same air we draw in we then give back to the universe, our life sustained by this communion.

In Sanskrit *hamsa* also has a second meaning: It is the word for a migrating bird, usually pictured as a swan or wild goose. In Heinrich Zimmer's words, this bird, the *hamsa*, "symbolizes the divine essence, which . . . remains forever free from, and unconcerned with, the events of individual life." We may be tethered to our preferences and aversions, our little habits, rituals, and fears. But inside, a wild bird—the *hamsa*—flies through the skies, leaving this all behind.

The migrating bird embodies a paradox. Of all creatures it seems least tethered to home. With a change of the weather, it is ready to set out on its travels, nary a glance back to be spared. Yet no other creature goes to greater lengths and perils to reach the comforts of home with its safe nest or abundant food. Each year, the arctic tern travels 25,000 miles from the Arctic to the Antarctic and back. It alone knows the vastness of our planet by encompassing it. Even lesser migrants, like varieties of geese, swans, and cranes, cover thousands of miles guided by the sun and stars, the earth's magnetic field, and memorized landmarks below. The *hamsa* lives out the "I am That" as it spans the heavens and earth.

Look deep within and you will find such a bird. It may be perched for a time, gobbling worms and making guano. But the season will change; the ancient urge arise; and your bird must finally take flight. Feel it spread its powerful wings. See its sensitive feathers shiver. Sense it rise on the air currents, skim the sea, climb level by level to crest the mountains, pierce through the clouds, and shine in the diamond-like sun. It matters not whether it flies with a brace of fellow travelers or, like the albatross, hovers alone. It is that part of you wild and free. That which longs for home so desperately that it wills to leave the only home that it has known and take to the limitless skies. So breathe deeply—hear *hamsa*—"I am That"—and bless that necessary journey.

When was the last time you felt that bird of spirit take to the skies? Do you sense a change of seasons; that it is time again to migrate? How might you best free that inner bird for flight?

Pretend You Are a Migrating Bird

BENEFITS: an experience of transcendence, of moving beyond the small self

Find a comfortable seated position; for example, sitting cross-legged on a cushion or firmly centered on a chair. Become aware of your breathing. Begin to hear, or softly voice in your mind, "hamsa" in time with the breath. On the in-breath hear *hum* (the "I"), as you follow the air into your heart-region in the center of your chest. On the out-breath, hear or think *sa,* pronounced "suh" (That), and mentally follow your breath as it travels out of your mouth or nose. Pause to imagine that exhaled air hovering a foot or two outside your body. Be with it for a moment before taking the next breath. You may begin to taste the "I am That" as you breathe into, then out of the self. This is a first stage of migration.

After a few minutes, begin to work explicitly with the second meaning of *hamsa* as migrating bird. Begin to imagine you are such a bird, and your breath is the flapping of your wings. On the in-breath (still hearing *hum*) feel your wings raise. On the out-breath (still hearing *sa)* feel your wings descend, propelling you through the skies. In the pause between breaths, feel yourself soar on the wind.

As you fly along on this breath of hamsa, you might imagine the landscape below. When you are ready for your meditation to end, visualize the place where you finally are coming to rest. Your long flight has brought you home.

Elemental Wisdom

We need to be open to the deep intelligence of
the world. We need to recognize the sacredness
of nature. And we begin by acknowledging that
matter itself—the very "stuff"
of the world, whether here on Earth or
elsewhere in the cosmos—tingles with
consciousness, sparkles with spirit.

CHRISTIAN DE QUINCEY,
CONTEMPORARY AUTHOR,
"STORIES MATTER, MATTER STORIES," IONS REVIEW #60

Rock

Being Strong, Sturdy, and Still

Take a rock's perspective for a change. Then you'll better see the changeless. Two lovers come along and sit on your back to engage in conversation. They come, they go, you remain. A butterfly alights on you and just as abruptly departs. There are dramatic changes of weather. You grow wet and slick from rain, then bake dry in the sun. You rest there by day, and through star-covered night, accepting everything as it is. You, the rock, are the fulcrum around which a turning world revolves.

Life changes. *"Anicca,"* the Buddhists call this process—the impermanent nature of all things. Happy circumstances give way to sad, and then reverse again unpredictably. Events, objects, jobs, people, come into our lives and then depart like passengers on a train who have made only the briefest of stopovers. We may not like this aspect of life, but there it is, unavoidable.

Yet imagine being a rock. Then there's nothing particular you have to *do*—cling, control, demand, fix. There's nothing particular you must *have* to guard against uncertain weather. All you need do is *be*—a rock. Then you can weather any storm, survive any mishap, witness all changes, yet ever sit still. You are weighty, solid, grounded.

Jesus, looking for a firm foundation for his teachings, places it on the back of a man he renames "Peter"—which in Latin means "rock." Acharya Vinoba Bhave, a Hindu teacher and follower of Gandhi, writes "It is only the stone that is fit to the image of the Lord. It is changeless, full of peace. Light or darkness, heat or cold, the stone remains the same."

This steadiness is also the rock's gift to others. You may have a friend who is anxious or grieving, confused by a turn of events. You don't need to run around and fix all their problems. More than anything they may need a rock.

Crossing a turbulent river, we leap from stone to stone, and so too those on a life-crossing. A young woman heads off to college. An older man faces serious illness. A long-standing relationship suddenly ends. Inner turmoil surfaces like a raging river. At such moments, yes, we need a rock—a trustworthy foothold, a strong, sturdy surface to step on amidst the change.

To be a rock for another can take many forms. You can listen on the phone. Give solid counsel. Hold a hand. Help with life tasks. Wipe away tears. In hard times a friend is rock-steady.

When has someone served as a rock for you? Is there someone in your life who could use that kind of help from you?

❖

Every particle of the world is a mirror,
In each atom blazes forth the light of a
thousand suns.
Open the heart of a raindrop and you
will find a hundred oceans.
In a grain of sand lies the seed of a
thousand beings.

MAHMUD SHABISTARI,
MEDIEVAL SUFI POET

❖

Sand

Harmonizing the Elements of Life

$S$and is a miraculous substance, the product of many elements sweeping through and transforming one another. It begins with solid rock, the earth element. But rock is worn down by wind and water, until the result participates in all three natures. Sand is stone, yet rendered airy and fluid. You can pour it from one hand to the other. It flies through the air, to the dismay of those who end up with grit in their eyes. The ripples of a sand dune echo the waves that ripple the ocean. Somehow it seems right for beaches to be made of sand, as if the fluidity of the sea has touched the land, turning it soft and yielding, liquid between our toes. On a hot day, the beach-sand even picks up the fiery warmth of the sun. Earth, air, water, fire—the classic elements of the ancient Greeks—are all wrapped together in sand.

No wonder children can play in it for hours, fascinated. Sand can be wetted down and—paradoxically becoming more solid from the addition of water—built into medieval-style castles. But such castles, historically massive and forbidding, in their sand-forms are delightfully fragile. A single wave and they're obliterated. Just to dig our hands into the sand feels special. It is abrasive (as in sandpaper), yet soft. Uniform beige, yet with glittery highlights. Flowing, yet granular. It's as if our skin, itself the meeting point of earth, air, body-heat, and blood-water, has found its natural kin.

Something in our soul also resonates with sand. We tend to attribute the peace we feel at a pristine beach to the sound and sights of the ocean. True, but let's not forget the seductions of sand. It invites us to grow smooth and relaxed. It awakens our sensuous, childlike nature. How can we engage in anything too serious on a beach? (Volleyball works, but not an important board meeting.) How can we be rigid and inflexible? Sand invites us to become like itself—soft, flowing, responsive to even the gentle breezes that surround us.

It takes many long years to turn a rock into sand. It can take as long to turn a stony person into a sandy one. Sometimes an unsolvable situation just keeps working away at us, wearing down our resistance. Finally, we soften and yield. We may see this sand-like character in the face of an elder, weathered by the changes of a lifetime. Her wrinkled face somehow suggests a soul that has grown smoother with the years. Her arms flow around a grandchild like sand. (The child can play gently, as he might in a sandbox, without pressures of time and duty.) When death finally arrives, this elder is ready to flow into the coffin like sand into a bucket. Life has worn her down, true, but in the process made her fine. She rests like sand along the shore of the ocean we call eternity.

Think about a troublesome situation in your life that has you a bit stymied. Are there any ways you are behaving in a stony fashion, rigid and inflexible? What might it mean to become more "sandy" within the situation —loose and flowing? (See if any new strategies come to mind for approaching things differently.

Sometimes I feel like the first being in one of our Indian legends. This was a giant made of earth, water, the moon, and the winds. He had timber instead of hair, a whole forest of trees. He had a huge lake in his stomach and a waterfall in his crotch. I feel like this giant. All of nature is in me, and a bit of myself is in all of nature.

JOHN (FIRE) LAME DEER,
SIOUX MEDICINE MAN

Pretend You Are Made of Sand

BENEFITS: deep physical and mental relaxation

Lay flat on your back on a comfortable surface (a bed is fine) with your arms and hands by your side, palms up. You may wish to use pillows to support your head and knees. Now pretend your body is filled with sand. Begin with your right leg, and imagine it to be a tube through which fine sand is flowing down and out your toes. Feel the sand dissolving and carrying away any tension. After a couple of minutes, go on to the left leg and imagine the same. Then do the same with each arm in turn—feel it as a hollow tube through which the sand is flowing down and out the fingers.

After doing the four limbs, do an inner scan of your torso, your shoulders, jaw and forehead. You'll notice places where you are holding tension. Imagine each as a kind of sand castle. Someone built and compacted the sand there into a structure. But imagine that structure now crumbling, as a sand castle collapses back into flowing sand. Feel that area of tension in your chest, jaw, or wherever, releasing back into fine sand.

Enjoy the sensations now filling your body. It is pleasurable to be made of sand.

Heat

The Energy of Life

*I*t's hard to truly appreciate heat unless you've been cold. Cold is a force that shrinks body and soul. When you're cold you huddle and shiver, drawing yourself together in a struggle (often fruitless) against the encroaching elements. Warmth, on the other hand, is expansive: We take off the sweater, loosen the necktie, relax, "let it all hang out." We speak about "warming up" to a topic or "growing hot around the collar." Again, whether meant positively or negatively, this refers to one's emotions expanding and expressing. Even our body does this in heat, as pores open, blood vessels dilate, and sweat presses out from our skin.

Finally, heat is the engine that powers the universe. The Big Bang, that explosion that created and dispersed all things, reached temperatures of 10^{32} degrees. When we fall in love, that is another sort of big bang: The heart grows warm and expands toward the other. In sexual intimacy, bodies rub and grow hot, a process that can produce a whole new body. And that fetal body must be kept warm in order to survive, for to grow too cold is to die.

This is true as well for our spiritual selves. We all too often have a tendency to let our souls grow cold. As with an untended fire, we are soon left with a pile of ashes and, if lucky, a glowing ember. Prayer, a good retreat, an inspiring book, can fan us back into flame. We feel our heart re-light with heat and passion. Soon we may even "burn" for God with a yearning that surprises.

When God said, "Let there be light," he might also have been saying, "Let there be heat." After all, light bears within it heat, and heat generates light. Both involve a sort of motion, and the emotion, that lie at the heart of life.

So appreciate the sun. And your furnace. A lit fire. Fossil fuels created from ancient dinosaur bodies. Your attic insulation. Your blanket. Your heartbeat. The metabolic energy of your cells.

Let us praise all that keeps us warm from outside and in, warm of mind, body, and soul. Today let us not take these forces for granted. It's good to be warm. Amen.

Today, take a few moments to appreciate your sources of warmth, physical, emotional, spiritual. Is there anything of yours (a relationship, a passion, a project) that has grown cold and needs to be re-ignited?

Gases
Lowering the Pressure

*W*hat happens when you take a gas and reduce the volume of its container? The pressure of the gas goes up, and therefore its temperature rises. This is the principle whereby a pressure cooker operates. Pressing the molecules together increases their kinetic energy and the heat they generate.

As in physics, so in human psychology. If you question this, just try your own experiment. Take your ordinary life with its vibrating molecules (the activities in which you are involved) and decrease the volume of the container. For example, decrease the amount of sleep you're getting each night. Or give yourself not quite enough time to complete everything on your to-do list.

Alternatively, find other ways to increase pressure on the system. Decide you must be the perfect parent, or to complete that project flawlessly at work. Increase the pressure created by your fear of failure; your need to please others; your anticipations of triumph or disaster.

As such forces press in, you will find that the laws which govern gases also govern the psyche. The system begins to vibrate more intensely and your mental temperature heats up. This will manifest in forms such as heightened anxiety, frustration, even rage. Look out—your pressure cooker may blow.

So what's the solution to all this stress? A physicist-psychologist might say: Simply expand the volume of the container. This creates more space for the molecules to bounce around in, allowing them to slow down. The whole system cools as kinetic energy descends. This manifests as mind-body relaxation.

Such an expansion happens when we give a pressing problem to God. The help comes not only from a subsequent divine intervention but from the act of prayer itself. We are placing our problem into a much larger container than that of the small ego-self. It now rests in the hands of the Infinite. We can begin to cool down.

So, too when we meditate, whatever technique we use—following the breath, visualizing a peaceful scene, or doing a movement yoga. We are no longer pressing to solve the problem but seeking to create a more spacious environment of mind, body, and spirit. Many a problem is not solved so much as *dis-solved* if given enough room to unfold.

There are many techniques of space-making. Going for a walk. Talking with a friend. Seeing the big picture. Deciding to eliminate unneeded commitments.

Of course, when a problem surfaces our first impulse is often to redouble our efforts, bearing down with clenched fists and furrowed brow. This may only serve to increase the mental strain. Remember instead that handy law of physics: To lower pressure, expand the volume.

In what ways do you "expand your volume," creating more space, relaxation, and mental freedom in your life? How might these help with any area where you currently feel a sense of pressure?

Water and Air

The Unseen Medium of Love

A fish is unaware of the water in which it swims. Similarly, we are unaware of the air we breathe despite the fact that, moment to moment, it sustains our very life. This is as it must be. A taken-for-granted medium allows us to focus on life's more specific challenges.

To a child, the love of the parent is like water to a fish—largely unnoticed, taken for granted. Not very often does the child turn to the parent and say, "Thank you for having me. For changing my poopy diapers, and coming to comfort me when I cried. For paying my dentist bills, for pasting Band-Aids on boo-boos. Thank you for all your support over the years—financial, physical, emotional. I'd have been like a fish flopping on dry land without the water of your love." Sounds great if you're a parent. But it ain't likely to happen, at least not until your children are well-grown, gone from the house, and able to view you a bit from the outside. When the fish swims inside you, it cannot notice.

This is true not only of parental love, but of filial love in general—that of family members for one another—and that for our truest friends. "Make new friends, but keep the old. One is silver and the other gold." So goes a ditty, but it may be truer to say that old friends are simply like air or water. They're just around us, sustaining us, circulating through our heart and mind. Hence, it's hard not to take those old friends for granted. In Joni Mitchell's words, "Don't it always seem to go that you don't know what you've got 'til it's gone?" The fish first discovers the existence of water when it is dragged, gagging, onto dry land. Often we come to value our loved ones most just after they're gone.

God is like a parent, religious traditions tell us, the loving Father or Mother. Or like a Friend to whom we can turn. And unlike our earthly parents and friends, who do die or move away, or prove destructively imperfect, we can eternally count on God.

But this can also account for why God so often seems absent. Yes, our very life is a holy mystery. Yes, somehow, in dark times, we find sustenance and strength. Yes, miracles of nature and the human spirit surround us. But this is all like the air we breathe, or water to a fish. And as a fish cannot locate water, so we cannot locate God. How can we see that which gives substance to our eyes, and every object we see, and all the spaces in between?

So next time you bemoan God's absence, realize this may be a disguised form of Presence. It is not that God is away on a business trip to other planets. It is not that God has abandoned or rejected you. The truth might be just the opposite: That God, like a loving parent, like water to a fish, is so accessible, so everywhere present, that God is nowhere to be found.

Today, spend a few minutes meditating in gratitude on the simple pleasures and miracles of the day you usually take for granted, and on the friends and family who surround you. Wake up to the air you breathe, the water in which you swim.

Ice and Snow

Miraculous Transformations

Follow a three-year-old through the day and you will meet many different creatures—a lion, a doggie, Batman, a doctor. A child lives in a fluid reality where beings can change form at a moment's notice. Going to the zoo she does not merely see, as a grown-up would, a bunch of animals. She discovers transmutational possibilities. That long-necked giraffe, fierce tiger, waddling penguin, are all beings she may become, and probably *will* as soon as she gets home.

But this is just pretend, isn't it? Maybe, maybe not. No, she doesn't really turn into a tiger. But maybe she's more attuned than adults to the truth of metamorphosis—that things can mysteriously transform into other things, exchange identities, invent themselves anew.

What more marvelous example than ice and snow? One minute there is water, a clear fluid running free. Then the cold casts its magic spell, and at a precise but mysterious moment (32 degrees Fahrenheit, but why just then?) presto change-o, everything is different. A mud puddle on a wintry day dons a Cinderella garment of crystalline ice. A rippling lake turns stone-solid. Raindrops that spatter against the face suddenly transform into slowly drifting flakes of snow, performing a leisurely cotillion that caresses the cheek. Is nature kidding, or what?

Yes, we know the scientific explanations. Still, they can't quite conceal the wizardry. How does water turn into ice and snow? How can elements so transform their nature? How does a little girl feel powerful as a lion at one moment, and at the next, like a scared mouse? How, for that matter, does day turn into night, summer into winter, toddler into grown-up? Change is everywhere, but ever a mystery.

Think of a time in your life when you underwent radical transformation like water into ice. Would you wish for any kind of transformation now? Are you willing to believe it possible, to work or pray for it?

Sacred Landscapes

Whenever in the course of the daily hunt, the red hunter comes upon a scene that is strikingly beautiful or sublime—a black thundercloud with the rainbow's glowing arch above the mountain; a white waterfall in the heart of a green gorge; a vast prairie tinged with the blood-red of sunset—he pauses for an instant in the attitude of worship.

OHIYESA (CHARLES ALEXANDER EASTMAN),
SIOUX AUTHOR, *THE SOUL OF THE INDIAN*

What I know of the divine science and Holy Scripture I learnt in woods and fields.

ST. BERNARD,
TWELFTH CENTURY DOCTOR OF THE CHURCH

The Outdoors

Our Truer Home

So much depends on whether we see ourselves as living indoors—venturing outside now and again—or as living outdoors, with recourse to indoor shelter. In the former case, human constructions are our home. A fluorescent-lit office space, the house we own or rent, a car by which we travel from one to the other—these are where we *dwell*. When need be, we are forced outside by the demands of an errand. We may even be seduced to wander by an unusually fine day, a planned outing, the wish to stretch our muscles. But these remain sojourns away from home which make it ever nicer to come back to our air conditioning and heating, electric lights and computers, stereos and TVs.

Don't get me wrong. I'm not putting these down. I enjoy such amenities of twenty-first century life. But when they become our primary reality amenities do not create the spirit of *amen*—awareness of the sacred. Dwelling in a human-made world, we are surrounded by *our* material goods, *our* technological advances, which shelter us but also close us in. The world that God breathed forth is something only glimpsed through a window whose solid panes keep out the wind.

How different it is to experience the outdoors as your true home. For roof there is the azure sky, stretching unto infinity and presenting an ever-changing play of sun and cloud, dawn and dusk, thunderstorms and gentle breezes. For floor—the moist earth, a firm foundation yet alive with trees, grass, and flowers, and the multitude of creatures that find there a home. Who could ask for a better carpet than mottled green grasses and mosses? For various rooms—the forest, ocean, meadow, mountain—the desert, swamp, and arctic ice. What interior decorator could come up with such a panoply of colors and forms, such a variety of moods?

To see yourself as living outdoors is to realize you dwell in the house of God. Why sell off this magnificent property to purchase a little hut?

So next time you walk out your door in the morning don't think you're leaving home. Say instead, "I'm entering my home." It was built the old-fashioned way with high-ceilings, sturdy floors, lots of living space, yet ample attention to detail. No home-owner could be prouder than you admiring this expansive domicile. Or more grateful to the Architect, Builder, and Landlord who freely handed you the keys.

When you venture outside today, see yourself as entering your wider home. See the trees as yours, the sky, the grass, and realize you inhabit the house of God.

❖

The pastures of the wilderness overflow, the hills gird themselves with joy, the meadows clothe themselves with flocks, the valleys deck themselves with grain, they shout and sing together for joy!

PSALM 65

❖

A Lake

Being Still Waters

"*He* leadeth me beside the still waters." Why is this line from the Twenty-Third Psalm such a well-loved and comforting image?

At first, "still waters" seems almost paradoxical. It is in the nature of water to flow, move, and change, the very opposite of stillness. A stone is still, not water, the stuff of crashing waves and tumbling streams. To be a fluid is, by definition, to be fluid—that is, in process, en route, outrunning boundaries.

We are watery, restless creatures. Life began in the ocean, and we hold a memory of the ocean within our salty blood. Our blood is 92 percent water, and our muscles and brain, 75 percent water. So, it seems, is our mind. It flows from one thought to the next, one emotion to the next, like a turbulent river or sudden rainstorm.

How to still our waters?—there's the question. How to grow quiet inside? How to be where we are, and not always racing toward a goal like a rushing river? When we become still enough our mental silt sinks to the bottom. This allows our awareness to clear. We are able to see deeper, as we could not when mud was swirling about the surface. "He leadeth me beside the still waters." Thank God when it happens and peace descends. The waters of our soul grow still.

Ever sit beside a lake? Its still waters do not exclude motion. A flock of geese may arrive trumpeting, and waddle about the shore. A passing breeze may ripple the pond skin. A bug may alight and use the water for a skating rink. Or a sudden fish jumps from the depths, shocking the scene alive. But the stillness of the lake absorbs all this. The lake sits quietly as if in meditation. Its heart is open. Its mind is peaceful. Its being rests in the depths.

Such are we when our soul grows still. Bugs aplenty—duties, disruptions, petty annoyances—alight upon our surface. A fish—an unconscious drive or desire—suddenly breaks into awareness. Our emotional weather shifts between clouds and sunshine. But through it all we remain still waters—deep, quiet, able to hold these changes without changing our character or losing our serenity.

Thoreau calls a lake,

> Sky water . . . It is a mirror which no stone
> can crack, whose quicksilver will never wear off,
> whose gilding Nature continually repairs; no
> storms, no dust, can dim its surface ever fresh;—a
> mirror in which all impurity presented to it sinks,
> swept and dusted by the sun's hazy brush.

WALDEN

The lake is a mirror reflecting the heavens above. And something like this happens when the soul becomes "still waters": It mirrors the clear light of the Divine.

Consider using the line "He leadeth me beside the still waters" as a repetitive prayer or meditation-focus. Use it to establish the mind of spacious awareness.

SHAPE-SHIFT
Pretend You Are a Lake

BENEFITS: growing still in mind and body and receptive to divine energy

Lie flat on your back on a comfortable surface (a bed is fine) with your arms and hands by your side, palms up. You may wish to use pillows to support your head and knees.

As your breathing begins to deepen, imagine that you are a lake. First feel your mud bottom. Allow your back, head, buttocks, and limbs to sink and relax as if they were made of mud. This will help you release any tension.

Now bring your attention to your lake-surface. Visualize that above you the sun is shining down. (Alternatively, you could be a lake at night—imagine the moon above.) Feel the sun warm your lake surface. Feel how perfectly you, in your stillness, reflect back that sun. Soon the sun above and the sun mirrored on your surface may almost seem to merge. Enjoy that feeling of reflecting and absorbing divine energy.

Distracting thoughts and sensations will arise. Imagine them as creatures of the lake that inevitably ruffle its stillness. For example, you might think of them as fish swimming through your depths, or bugs alighting on your surface. The lake does not reject any of its creatures. Don't reject your thoughts or feelings. Nonetheless, keep returning your focus to the greater lake and the sun (or moon) above. Feel yourself again become still waters.

Note: You might add to this meditation by visualizing a lotus flower, or other water lily, resting on your surface in your heart region. Feel it open its petals to absorb the sun's rays. (In the Hindu and Buddhist traditions, the lotus is a symbol of enlightened consciousness for though its roots lie deep in the muck it grows upward to the surface, culminating in a flower of great beauty.)

The Desert

The Gifts of Desolation

*T*he desert bears within it a spare beauty. The sun rises to illuminate a terrain stunning yet desolate. Even the colors are spare—a subtle palette of red, brown, and sand hues—with the occasional smudge of purple or pink streaking the sky or a flower. Most of all, the desert is spacious—open—empty—in a way that expands our being. The desert invokes the mind of Buddha, silent and aware.

No wonder the early fathers of Christian monasticism repaired to the desert to repair their souls. And no wonder the desert landscape is sacred to Native American tribes who use it as a site for vision quests. The desert is the place we go to be alone—not alone in the sense of holing up in an apartment—but the aloneness that carries us into a wholeness greater than that of the self.

So we must not shy away from deserts. Forbidding as they seem, they come bearing gifts that cannot be found elsewhere. A forest surrounds us with lush, vernal luxury. A mountain summons us to view the big picture. A river offers the coolness and fluidity that helps us to glide through life. But in a desert we simply *are*. The stiller we become, like a lizard on a rock, the larger we expand.

What seems to be depression can be a desert experience if we are willing to sit with it. The loss of a valued relationship leaves us feeling *deserted*. Or our plans go wrong, and we feel the suffering that follows to be our just *desert*. The failure of a dream, the death of a loved one, the experience of our own aging and mortality—there we are again, sitting in the desert. Empty. Desolate. Alone. The temptation is to fill up the landscape with distractions, as if the Mojave would be more tolerable with a hastily erected amusement park. Drink, sex, work, drugs, TV: we'll turn anywhere for relief.

But what if instead we let the desert be desert? Rest silently in the emptiness. Experience the parched landscape. The flat mesas. The prickly cactus. Paradoxically, here in the unrelieved heat may be where the healing is found. The cactus contains within it hidden moisture. Its tough skin and needles are a sign of its strength, its determination to survive harsh circumstances. And at the right moment—to our amazement—blossoms the cactus flower, vibrant and alive.

If anything is depressing you at the moment, instead of fighting that experience go into it, at least for a brief time. Let the feelings of desolation or loneliness emerge. Sit in the desert, knowing that this too can be a place of healing.

Mountains

The Spiritual Ascent

*C*limb a mountain—in your mind. Your trek starts out at the mountain's base, which is nothing other than the earth itself, but beginning to reach up to heaven like hands joined in prayer. Yet these are also open hands: The base of the mountain is broad, inviting, with many trails leading to the peak. In fact, *all* trails from the base will carry you upward. The obstacle lies not in the mountain, but in the self. Are you willing to leave your home village, the comforts of the familiar?

Once committed to the trip, the mountain itself becomes your guide. It escorts you up like a friend who holds your hand. It challenges you to battle gravity, the weight of all that anchors you to earth. It signals to you through outward shifts of terrain the inward shifts that are called for. The air grows cooler, more spacious—so, too, shall your mind. The sky stretches overhead like a blank canvas across which clouds flow and disappear. So, too, is the inner sky of awareness unsullied by thoughts that come and go. As you ascend, the tree cover grows more sparse. So, too, thins the forest of your worldly preoccupations, the brambles of sin and desire. Ascending, you encounter bare rock: It is time for the soul to bare itself. Can you bear to see the naked truth? Near the mountaintop the wind howls its presence. It means to blow through you, opening every pore so you can fully heed its call.

Finally, you reach a point of ice and snow. From whence comes this purity? Such whiteness is not a product of the world beneath but a gift from heaven. The clouds that embrace the peak are like ice made airy. A stream cascades down from a spring snow melt. Heaven's gifts are not isolated but water the world below.

Finally, with a last tired step you reach the mountain's peak. No wonder we speak of the "peak experience." In every direction space falls away forever. The valley of care from which you climbed is but a small thing sighted from this lofty perspective. You stand alone in the solitude of the One.

The trip down is bound to be anticlimactic, a somewhat running and stumbling journey through already traveled terrain, downward toward precisely that patch of earth from which you had so longed to be free. But if you are lucky . . . and mindful . . . you will bring back with you a piece of the mountain. Re-entering your daily affairs, you will retain your mountain-mind—spacious, lofty, far-sighted, yet ever connected to the earth.

For the mountain is the bridge between earth and heaven, dirt and sky, our humanity and our divinity. Whenever you lose that connection then it's time to climb a mountain. At least climb a mountain in your mind.

If you were to climb an inward mountain, what sort of life problems and frustrations would you rise above? From that loftier perspective, what might you see? (Solutions to your problems, or that they're not that big a deal? Larger life-issues you've been neglecting?) See the big picture from the mountaintop.

Pretend You Are a Mountain

BENEFITS: a sense of grounded power, of enhanced equanimity amidst life's changes

Sit down in a well-grounded way. This may involve sitting cross-legged on a couch or the floor. Alternatively, sit in a chair with your back straight, though not rigid, your feet resting firmly on the floor. The key is to find a seated position that feels strong, erect, well-balanced.

Now imagine you are a mountain. You are not just sitting *on* the earth, like a detachable object. You *are* the earth, thrusting upward. As such, feel your buttocks firmly rooted on your seat like the mountain's base. Feel in the length of your spine the mountain's dignity and height. Sense your torso as the broad and stable mountain-body.

As you inhale and exhale, experience your breath as the winds that circulate around a mountaintop. Whatever moods you pass through during the meditation, imagine them as the changing weather that surrounds the peak. Sometimes it is sunny or rainy. The mountain accepts all and is fundamentally unchanged. Whether happy, sad, or anxious feelings arise, accept them with the same equanimity.

Deal similarly with passing thoughts and sensations. See them as clouds that come and go. Or imagine them as birds circling your mountaintop, squawking. Don't drive them off. Imagine the birds flying away on their own accord, or alighting on the mountain and thereby disappearing from view.

Even in the midst of a changing world, the mountain remains timeless and serene.

Note: As you breathe, you might want to consciously bring the air into your abdomen or chest, and imagine it as a wind entering and leaving a mountain cave. Visualizing a cave in your belly can bring about deep relaxation. Breathing instead into your chest will help activate what the Hindus call the "cave of the heart."

Polar Exploration
Striving Toward the Ultimate

*W*hy are we so fascinated with arctic journeys? Why did Scott, Peary, Amundsen, Byrd, and so many others who lived and died in the attempt, set out for the North or South Poles? And why do we love to read of their exploits while lying on the living room sofa?

The explorer's journey speaks to the universal journey of soul that dimly calls to us all. First, there is the element of renunciation. Heading into an arctic region involves stripping oneself bare. Most of one's possessions, and the desires that provoked them, must be abandoned. Otherwise they weigh heavily and doom one's journey. And so, too, on the spiritual path do we need to free ourselves from the crasser pulls toward money, selfish pleasure, career advancement, that weigh us down. It is not that we have to renounce all these aspects of the "good life." We do, however, need to renounce our addictiveness, which places such drives first in our life, rather than our search for Spirit.

As we journey beyond these things our inner world begins to purify. We see a visual image of this in the arctic landscape. It has a strange and other-worldly beauty, a mystical grandeur. This is not the beauty of the verdant forest, the lush meadow, nature in all its soft profligacy. No, this is nature stripped bare—snow-white and ice-covered. The bleached skeleton is revealed beneath fleshy nature. So, too, on the inner exploration do we encounter a landscape stripped bare, sometimes devoid of consolations, but compelling in beauty.

The journey is hard but once entered into, we must keep going. To stop is to die. There are austerities to observe, rigors to survive, but the reward is the greatest imaginable: to achieve the Pole. It exerts a magnetic pull on the human soul just as it does on a compass. We must get there. We are drawn onward. We hardly know why.

What is the Pole? Clearly it is not just a geographical locale, but more like a state of Being. The place where all longitudes meet. Where all that was dispersed joins in unity. The ultimate. Peary's party, for example, trekked north, and north, and north toward its destination, but on reaching the North Pole found there is no more north. This is IT. Every direction surveyed becomes southerly, dispersive. They reached the *omphalos*, point of origin and completion, the great white Navel of the World.

A Buddhist mantra is *Gate, Gate, Paragate, Parasamgate, Bodhi Svaha*—Gone, gone, gone beyond, gone beyond the beyond, all hail the enlightened one! And we must hail the man or woman who reaches the Pole. He or she has gone beyond self, beyond the everyday world, beyond all human limits. Through the exertion of courage, physical effort, and discipline, acumen, teamwork, and compassion, the explorer has purified the self and reached the Pure Place—the Alpha and Omega, the One.

The Pole then is nothing less then a symbol of God. To reach God, we must be tested, reach within, and transcend. The Pole and Polar explorer are necessarily linked.

When such a person returns there is much that can be shared—photos, scientific discoveries, tales of danger and inspiration. In a sense such a person has reached the Pole on behalf of all—just as a Buddha, or Jesus, or a realized saint embraces us all by their labors.

Still, the explorer but shows the way. He or she cannot transport us there. We must finally set out from our too-comfortable home and undertake our own journey. Not to the geographic North or South Pole: That would be taking a metaphor to the extreme. But to search for the Pole within—the point of unity, and union with God—is an adventure that calls to us all.

Ask yourself, toward what goal or goals are your life-energies pointing? Are such goals rich and significant enough? What would be the highest "pole" to seek, and what austerities and commitments are needed for that journey?

The Natural World
Moving Beyond Moralities

*S*ince time immemorial people have projected their moral codes onto a King of the heavens. So many have uttered some variant on the following: "I will strike you down in the name of God, because thou dost offend his Righteousness and call down His anger, of which I am the instrument."

Jesus takes a different tack: "But I say to you, love your enemies and pray for those who persecute you, so that you may be children of your Father in heaven; for he makes his sun rise on the evil and on the good, and sends rain on the righteous and on the unrighteous" (Matthew 5:44–45). Here Jesus is saying something like: *"Get off it."* God is not a cosmic tyrant, holding the same self-righteous prejudices we do. The evidence? Simply look at the world God made. There is sun and rain. Both are necessary for crops to flourish. But they are not offered or withheld according to moral worth, as many of us would do if masters of the universe. The righteous farmer is not given a bit more sunshine to ripen his grapes, or a timelier downpour when drought threatens, while the sinner's crops are left to parch. Anyone who thinks this is how the universe works is a poor observer of the natural world and hence a poor theologian.

In the words of the Chinese Tao te Ching:
The great Tao flows everywhere,
both left and right.
All beings depend upon it;
it rejects no one.
It silently fulfills its purpose, making no claims.

(#34)

Not even a claim that we must be good.

When will we come to terms with this scandal—that Creation,

bountiful and balanced as it may be, is not about "good" and "bad"? What a scandal, but also what a relief. Haven't we all had enough of conditional love, which our well-meaning parents lavished or withheld depending on their judgment of our conduct? "You were so polite, let me give you a kiss!" Or, "You were rude, march right to your room!" Hey, it's part of the parent's job to use a bit of Pavlovian conditioning (kisses, banishment) to elicit civilized conduct. But can we reduce the Creator of one hundred billion galaxies to a sort of eat-your-peas prig?

Many religious teachers have tried to do so: eat your (moral) peas, and you can have infinite dessert (heaven); don't and you'll be sent to your room forever (hell). Thankfully, the universe is more subtle and less judgmental than this. The skies, rivers, and mountains don't watch our every move and punish the least transgression.

True, our actions have natural consequences. Certain modes of being (like kindness, acceptance, humility) are more in harmony with the Tao, and thus help us to flourish. Conversely, "That which goes against the Tao comes to an early end" (Tao te Ching, #30). Behave selfishly, as if only you existed, and you'll likely find yourself at a crucial juncture frustrated and friendless. It would be like a plant separating off from the surrounding ecosystem and growing sickly as a result.

So nature is a teacher, but not a self-righteous one. After all, sun and rain, ever bountiful, give themselves equally to saint and sinner. It is a spirit to which we can aspire.

Are you hanging onto some self-righteous judgments about others? See if you can't loosen up on one or more. You might visualize sending a troublesome person sunshine from your heart.

Wilderness

A Wildness Beyond the Self

*H*uman beings have a persistent fascination with wilderness. For us more sedentary twenty-first century folks this often plays out vicariously: reading or watching movies about doomed arctic expeditions, unearthly storms, impossible mountain treks, journeys to the heart of the savage wild. What is so alluring about inhospitable locales? What is it in the human soul that pulls us, time and again, into places not fit for human habitation?

Isn't it precisely their forbidding nature that makes them so fascinating? They speak of a world transcendent to our own. In the story of Job he starts out expecting a village-god who, like the local magistrate, should run an orderly town and reward him for good behavior. Job complains when God seems to do otherwise. But he roars back from the whirlwind, "Have you entered into the springs of the sea, or walked in the recesses of the deep? Who has cut a channel for the torrents of rain, and a way for the thunder-bolt, to bring rain on a land where no one lives, on the desert which is empty of human life. . . . Do you know when the mountain goats give birth? Do you observe the calving of the deer? . . . Is the wild ox willing to serve you? Will it spend the night at your crib? . . . Is it at your command that the eagle mounts up and makes its nest on high?" That is, in the vast scheme of things, *who the heck are you?*

Job's kvetching (whining and complaining) falls silent. All that's left is his humble concession: "Therefore I have uttered what I did not understand, things too wonderful for me which I did not know."

To a degree, we're all Job. We fall victim to the delusion that the world, even God, is there to serve our demands. While it's comforting to think of a universe so benignly designed, it's not quite realistic. When things go bad we're likely to rail against a betraying God and feel our faith collapse. This faith, from the start, was in something too small, a little idol to place on the night-stand beside our bed. From time to time, we need to be reminded that God is also the God of the *unfathomable*: a hundred billion galaxies each with a hundred billion stars. Even the Earth, that planet ideally suited to our life, contains the polar ice-caps, track-less seas, forbidding peaks, savage wilderness. This reminds us, like Job, to shut up, bow our heads, and marvel at the mystery.

So when we go out hiking, or read the latest saga of death-defying treks or deadly sea-storms, we are not only searching for adventure. We are also searching for the Voice—the voice in the whirlwind. Like Job, we need to know that God is there for us, but also, in a sense, that God is not. The universe is not. Even the Earth is not. Only then, realizing our smallness, can we open to the Wonder of the Wild.

Today use something to remind yourself of the unfath-omable vastness and wildness of the world; look at a nature photo, read from a book on wilderness, gaze up at the sky . . . and let that become your worship.

❖

There was a time when meadow, grove,
and stream,
The earth, and every common sight,
To me did seem
Appareled in celestial light,
The glory and freshness of a dream.

WILLIAM WORDSWORTH,
"INTIMATIONS OF IMMORTALITY
FROM RECOLLECTIONS OF EARLY CHILDHOOD"

❖

Two

Object Lessons

What Our Things Have to Teach Us

The Car, a Spiritual Guide

One who does not see the Omnipresent in every place will not see Him in any place."

MENAHEM MENDEL,
NINETEENTH CENTURY HASIDIC TEACHER

Driving

Lessons for the Highway of Life

*D*riving is a lesson in *humility*. We wish the world were built to satisfy our every need. There should be no red lights facing our direction, only green. The roads should be cleared of excess cars that might constitute an impediment for us. Surprise! As soon as we begin to drive we are disabused of this delusion. We must wait at lights, take turns with other drivers, cope with traffic jams. Whether in a sub-compact or a pricey limousine we share the road equally with countless others. Where else does such democracy rule?

Driving is a lesson in *self-honesty*. We may take pride in our kind and generous nature but don a cloak of anonymity (since you do not know the other drivers, or they, you) and the beast within emerges. We may find ourselves honking, cursing, and falling into all kinds of sexist, racist, classist, and ageist forms of stereotyping and condemnation. Love thy neighbor? Hah! Not on the highway. Road rage is more like it, for this one drives too slow, delaying us with her dilly-dallying, and that one is too fast, riding our tail like a macho cowboy. Terrible drivers, each and every one. It rarely occurs to us that our neighbors, blessed with the self-same mentality, think we are the bad drivers.

Driving is a lesson in *prudence*. Finally, we must deal with the reality that the road does not belong to us alone—that we must accept our neighbor, adjust to his or her patterns. We must or else we die. In ordinary life, we can steamroll others. Get out of my way, bud, I'm coming on through. Try that on the road, and you risk substantial expense, inconvenience, bodily injury, even death. If driving gives license to our insane side, it also provokes communal sanity in order to preserve life and limb.

So next time you're driving, realize there's no better spiritual exercise—no better way to *exorcise* your demons of impatience, pride, and selfishness. Can you accept your neighbor; be courteous and giving; forgive the faults of others; be humble about your own skills and tendencies; work well with fellow drivers to facilitate everyone's progress; meet life's red lights and traffic jams with equanimity; and know that it matters little to arrive a few moments early, but it matters much that the journey be good? To learn to drive well is to learn how to live.

When you next drive notice what triggers your frustration and why. Using whatever aids you wish (such as prayer, deep breathing, focused intent, soft music) try to practice a bit more patience and courtesy than you otherwise might. See how the quality of your journey changes.

Cars

A Teacher of Self-Care

*I*f we drove ourselves the way we drive our cars, we'd probably make out better. Why? The simple truth is that we likely treat our car more considerately than we do ourselves. Being a dumb machine, the performance of our vehicle will be directly tied to our handling of it. If we let it run out of gas, the car stops. If we hurtle everywhere in overdrive, the engine burns out. If we neglect periodic maintenance, the car will drive sluggishly, and be more likely to develop serious problems which then demand costly repairs. All this reminds us to service the damn thing in at least the rudimentary ways.

Not so, ourselves. Sometimes it seems we can get away with it, whether "it" means little sleep, overwork, poor eating habits, or equally slipshod thinking habits involving worry, gripes, and obsession about trivia. No wonder at times we perform sluggishly. Run out of gas. Burn up our bodies prematurely, courting collapse.

We're not giving ourselves even the routine care we usually accord our car.

So forget about yogis from the mysterious East. Your best and most holistic teacher may be none other than your car. My guru, the Subaru? Let's listen to its guidance.

First (the car might say) pay attention to your fuel. Any car needs gas to run, and the higher the octane, the better your performance. So do you remember to eat right through the day? (Okay, this car is a bit of a nudge.) Not only physical food, but also the emotional and spiritual kinds? When I get low on gas (the car talking) we pull over to a gas station to fill up the tank. What is your human equivalent—pulling over to rest, to pray, have fun, or call a friend? When your tank is near empty how do you gas up?

And let's also talk about shifting gears. It's nice to zoom along on a superhighway. If I do that on a smaller street I'm going to crash and burn. Do you downshift when appropriate? To be with the kids. To work through a problem. At night, or the weekend, when it's time to relax. To take a few moments, even on a busy day, to notice the roadside scenery. I see humans (the car says) always stomping on the accelerator. You seem to have trouble knowing when to brake, that is, when to take a break and slow down.

While we're at it, you humans neglect regular maintenance. If I'm going to last ten years my car-body needs tune-ups and servicing. Aren't you hoping to preserve your body for seventy or eighty years or more? Good luck—luck does play a part in it. But so does routine service and maintenance. For humans, there's daily exercise and a good night's sleep. Avoiding poisons likely to clog up your engine. Then the periodic tune-up—a doctor's visit, vacation, or retreat.

So every time you stop at a gas station, car wash, or garage it's a great reminder to *do the same for yourself*. Why take better care of your car than of yourself?

Ask yourself some of the questions mentioned above: How do you fill up your tank during the day? Are you shifting gears when needed? Are you attending to the maintenance of body and soul? You might write up an "owner's manual" of best practices for yourself, as manufacturers include with their cars.

Windshield Wipers
The Practices That Clear Our Vision

*W*e all need windshield wipers when driving on a rainy day. The rain interferes with our vision, creating a potential hazard on the road. Fortunately, we have a mechanism that automatically, repetitively, continuously, reliably, clears the glass. The wipers do not call attention to themselves. That would be distracting. Their job is to allow us to see beyond to the highway.

We also need windshield wipers on the highway of life. Rarely does a day go by without a rain of little annoyances, major setbacks (at least they feel major in the moment), distressing world events, or our own neuroses. Pretty soon we're likely to lose sight of the "road"– the Tao, the way of harmony. Before we know it we end up in a ditch or having a head-on collision with another driver. We all need "windshield wipers"—the disciplines that clear our vision and help us to stay on track.

Members of the Jesuit order are encouraged each evening to perform an "examen of conscience." Where has God manifested in the events of the day? Where have we responded, and where fallen short? This help clears away the day's murk and drizzle, allowing us to better see the Divine.

Similarly, a recovering alcoholic uses the daily "tenth step" of the Twelve Step program to catch developing problems. It has questions such as: Was I resentful, selfish, dishonest or afraid? Do I owe an apology? What could I have done better? What corrective measures or amends need I make? Each honest answer—swish, swish—is a wiper cleaning up the mess.

Meditation is a wonderful mind-cleaner. In the face of anger, lust, or confusion, to be able to sit down and do nothing—simply observe one's own mental processes in a neutral fashion, or focus on the breath going in and out—begins to create a zone of clarity. One regains a spacious awareness not occluded by emotion's smear.

Such windshield wipers abound. Faith traditions offer more varieties than a well-stocked auto supply store. Give your problem to God in prayer. Repeat your mantra. Turn to scripture for answers. Chant and sing. Bare your soul in confession. Honor the Sabbath. In such ways we wipe away some of the muck which besets even the best-lived life.

Of course, some of the nicest windshield wipers are personal, and, at least on the face of it, secular. You might call a best friend to bitch and moan, then seek advice, laugh, and reflect. Another person sets off for a walk in the woods. A third sees a therapist, processing ancient hurts and their daily triggers. Another puts on loud music and dances until dawn.

In a three-ton high-speed vehicle the most important part might be that bit of rubber and plastic—the wipers. Don't try maneuvering in a rainstorm without them. And don't try driving the highway of life without a deep breath, a prayer, a good cry, or whatever else wipes your windshield.

Ask yourself, what are your personal windshield wipers? Are they working well or is it time to replace them? And when you most need them do you remember to switch them on? (It's easy to forget to do so when the rain seems overwhelming, and we're scared to let go, even for a moment, of the wheel.)

In the biblical perspective there are not two distinct worlds, the profane and sacred. Everything is sacred.

PAUL TOURNIER,
THE ADVENTURE OF LIVING

SHAPE-SHIFT
Pretend You Have Windshield Wipers

BENEFITS: enhanced calmness and insight during turbulent times

Have a seat. Begin by imagining you are driving a car. Allow any thoughts, worries, feelings, sensations that have been troubling you to arise. Image them as rain falling, mind-rain, so to speak. This rain can cloud your vision, making it difficult to see the road. Is this a turbulent thunderstorm or a gentle drizzle? See the mind-rain that is impeding your life journey.

Now imagine turning on your windshield wipers. Use a simple repetitive stimulus of your choosing. You might work with a "mantra" or repeated prayer. Almost all the religions of the world have their version, or you can make up your own. For example, you might say "shalom," the Hebrew word for peace, the first syllable on the in-breath, the "om" on the out-breath. If Christian you might use the name, "Jesus," if Muslim, "Allah," etc. You can also work with a simple formulation, like "all shall be well," "peace," or "God is."

Alternatively, you can simply use the in and out of the breath as your mental focus.

Repeat this mantra, or your gentle breathing, over and over, so that it becomes like the repetitive swishing of windshield wipers. Whenever your mind returns to a problem, worry, or distraction, think of it as rain falling on your windshield. Use your windshield wipers. That is, return your focus to your prayer or breathing and let this clear your mind again.

A nice way to end the meditation is to imagine that, thanks to your wipers, you have successfully driven all the way home. Imagine yourself pulling up to a home of your imagining (or some other inspiring place). Amidst the rain, you have successfully negotiated the road of life and reached your destination.

Note: When things get hairy (rainy) during the day, and you begin to feel out of control emotionally, or unable to locate the right path, remember to turn on your windshield wipers. Spend a few moments with your mantra or breathing and let them clear your vision.

Speed Bumps
Progress Through Slowing Down

Speed bumps can be awfully frustrating if you're in a hurry. Misnamed, they are actually *anti-speed bumps* designed to slow you down. Still, they are there for good reason. The racing motorist may be a danger to himself and others, and speed bumps tend to lessen that threat.

The proverbial road of life is filled with bumps. But do we realize how many of these may be speed bumps in disguise? Say you're zooming through your days in overdrive when you're pulled up by a bad back. The pain is annoying but it forces you to slow down, rest, then do some stretching and exercise. Certain demands of home and business are necessarily put on hold as you seek to diminish your stress. These shifts in lifestyle may prove healing and pleasant. If sustained, they may even save your life, protecting you from future disease.

Or say your career hits a bump. You were counting on a promotion but your company had other ideas. At first, disappointment reigns. You brood and plot revenge. You feel blocked, sidetracked, or at a dead end.

But pretty soon a new opportunity opens up that you hadn't quite expected. Your work life takes a new turn, and you're back on track, albeit headed in a different direction. Of course, to make that turn successfully you first had to slow down. If it hadn't been for the speed bump (that promotion you didn't get) you would have raced on obliviously and missed that new job.

On life's path there are job bumps, health bumps, love bumps, bumps in our emotional and spiritual development. It all makes for a choppy ride and many a loose axle. We may curse the road. Who did this shoddy work? Or we may condemn our vehicle or our driving skills as deficient. Don't the best drivers just speed along?

hey did they would miss so much: roadside stands,
_cenery, key turning points on the way to undreamed-
of destinations. Thankfully, the road of life is no autobahn, but
filled with speed bumps to slow us down. That's often how we
make the quickest progress.

What speed bumps have come into your life in the past?
Can you see benefits from how they've slowed you down
or facilitated shifts in direction? Can you see the potential
for this in speed bumps you are now encountering?

The Passenger Seat
Surrendering Control

"*P*ut God in the driver's seat." It's an old cliché, but with
substance. Climb on over to the passenger seat and the ride
gets so much smoother.

Imagine yourself the "driver" in one of those arcade games
that places you behind the wheel of a super-charged sports car.
With effort and skill you can stay on the road for a time, but the
turns come fast and furious, the car accelerates as if of its own
accord, and sooner or later (usually sooner) you crash against a
wall, or smash into an oncoming truck. True, your little car rights
itself (unless your three minutes are up) and revs again onto the
main road, but the subsequent results are likely to be the same. It's
a thrilling ride—perhaps worth the fifty cents—but it can also
leave you stressed out and frustrated. That's the fun/not fun of
the game.

How many days have that video game feel? You're racing against a deadline, running up against unexpected obstacles (a harried boss? a moody spouse? a child who simply won't get dressed?). As you try to motor through the sharp curves you spin the wheel left or right, step on the accelerator, or slam the brakes. But sooner or later you're likely to have a wreck. It's rare to circumnavigate the track without crashing into somebody, or crashing inside.

How much smoother it goes when God, Spirit, the Inward Voice (whatever you choose to call it) is at the wheel. We clamber over to the passenger seat and relax, knowing the trip is in good hands. Instead of racing forward in self-will we pause to breathe, meditate, ask for guidance. We let a Higher Power direct our thoughts and actions.

Everything then begins to slow down. The road itself seems a little straighter, its curves more gradual and well-banked. Maybe this is just the artifact of a better driver at the wheel. We experience a calmer ride, as if tooling down a highway, but one with frequent rest stops, and pleasant detours that lead onto tree-lined streets. We're getting somewhere, yet also enjoying the trip. How different than racing around a track which, for all its frenetic motion, never really leads anywhere.

So surrender the wheel, the mystics say. Surrender for the sake of your serenity.

How often do you feel like your vehicle is "Higher Powered," guided by God at the wheel? When and why do you seize control? Are you willing to experiment with slipping over to the passenger seat?

Openings and Closings

Ask, and it shall be given you; seek, and ye
shall find; knock, and it shall be opened unto you.

NEW TESTAMENT, MATTHEW 7:7

Good fences make good neighbors.

TRADITIONAL PROVERB

Opening and Shutting Doors
The Benefits of a Good Barrier

A door is truly an amazing thing. Closed, it is an agent of separation. It completes a wall that divides off two rooms, or the inside of a house from the outside. But swing it open and it becomes an invitation, uniting what before was separate. Suddenly you can see and walk through one space into another. They are married by the open door.

The human body, come to think of it, is filled with doors. The breath swings in and out through nose and mouth. The oxygen so gained then crosses membranous doors into our lungs and red blood cells. Our blood then passes through swinging-door heart valves on its way to feed the rest of the body. This it does when, at just the right moment, cellular doors open to release oxygen to the tissues. Yes, our body is doors upon doors, both macro- and microscopic. All life needs doors that swing shut to guard the organism but open to allow for exchange.

Is the psyche any different? Crucial for our mental stability are doors that can open. We need to open our mind to new ideas, our heart to the troubles of others. We need to open our mouth to speak when appropriate, and our ears to listen. Pity the close-minded person, the egomaniac, and those who are too withdrawn. Such people have psychic doors stuck shut. The room of the self grows musty.

But just as we suffer from a door frozen shut, so from a door left too long open. Too much chatter, stimulation, distraction, and demand leave us feeling played out and depleted. There is a time to cease talking and sit in silence. To withdraw from company and rest within the self. To shut the door even on the chattering of our own mind, which can be worse than that of a roomful of blowhards. Be quiet. Be alone. Be still.

Then a funny thing may happen. In that closed room, the soul withdrawn into itself, there appears a mysterious guest. Call it God, the Holy Spirit, or one's own True Self long forgotten and made a stranger. We sense a presence. In the depths of solitude we are no longer lonely but feel more whole and connected. Are we then closing a door or opening one? Yes.

Have you shut the door lately, separated off from the world, to reconnect with your inward self? How might you make time and space to do this? Might this help you open your heart to God or to others?

Unlocking With a Key
Penetrating the Barriers of Life

A key is not just a thing: It's also a powerful metaphor. We speak of the "key to the problem," or "the key to understanding," and that finding such keys will help us "unlock" solutions. We may even forget that we're using a metaphor because it fits so well. Why? Let's try to unlock this metaphor.

Reference to a key implies recognition of a barrier. A door, a box, a closet is locked shut. Fairy tales are filled with these, and so, in a sense, is life. We can't resolve the mounting tension between a parent and a child. We are baffled by a computer problem. Relations between two countries continuously deteriorate. The way out of such problems, be they trivial or global, seems blocked. All that keeps us going is the faith that somehow, somewhere must lie a solution. This is like a locked door, not an impenetrable wall, and it can be opened if we find the key.

But this proves no easy matter. Any lock, after all, is built to hide its solution. Imagine a safe with a combination lock whose answer (12 to the left, 15 to the right, 24 to the left) were posted on its surface. The lock would then be no use at all, the "safe" radically unsafe. No, the answer must be concealed. Similarly, the particular serrations and angles that release a key-lock are hidden inside, invisible, leaving us excluded and baffled.

Sometimes things feel like that. We reach for what to say to an angry spouse, what shifts need be made in a marriage. More honesty? Or tactfulness? More self-assertion, or less? More time and activities apart, or more togetherness? We flip through the keys, but cannot tell which one will release the recalcitrant lock.

Still, we persist. If we are sincere in our efforts—if in our actions we manifest willingness to change—if in our humility, we consult with others and with God, the master Locksmith—we are likely to finally find the key.

When this happens it is magical. A tiny key slides into place, turning a larger bolt, releasing a massive door, which opens up a new world.

Perhaps that key was small as a moment of kindness. A word of forgiveness. An admission of wrongdoing. An inspiration. A chance encounter. A heartfelt prayer. And, lo, the mighty door swung open.

The Tao te Ching describes the Tao, creative energy of the universe, as incomparably great, yet also "very small" (Tao te Ching, #34). For "the soft and weak overcome the hard and strong" (Tao te Ching, #36). Water wears down rock. Gentleness wins over resistance. The tiny thing penetrates the huge barrier.

So never despair, in life, or in prayer. The forces that block and trouble us are mighty as a fortress. By comparison, the forces of salvation seem small. And so they are—but they are small like a key.

What problems or barriers do you currently face that need to be "unlocked?" Imagine that where there is a block there is also a key. Allow your intuitive mind to suggest possibilities for what that key might be.

Benefits: insight and inspiration in relation to life in general, or specific issues.

Take a seat, and a few moments to breathe, relax, and center. Now visualize yourself as at the foot of a set of stairs leading upward. Imagine that with each breath you ascend one step, climbing ten steps in total to the next landing. (Or instead you might imagine yourself descending down a stairway—this can take you into subconscious depths.) Now see yourself walking down a corridor, again taking ten steps, one to a breath. Finally, you have come to a door. Next to the door is a table on which sits a key. This can be any sort of key that you imagine—small or large, modern, or old-fashioned and ornate.

Notice that above the door a word or words are written. It might be a word like "joy," or "wisdom," a general trait that you wish to understand and live more fully. Or the word(s) might label a more specific issue like "healing in my marriage."

Now pick up the key and insert it in the door. It works! The lock releases and the door swings open. You are able to enter the room. Inside it you will find symbols and images of that which was named above the door—"joy," or "wisdom," or whatever. You may find an object, or series of objects. You may see a specific scene unfold. You might find yourself in a natural setting or engaged in a certain activity. Without judgment, see what this magical room has to show you about "wisdom," or whatever attribute you chose to explore.

When you are ready to leave feel free to take something with you as a reminder of what you have learned. This might be an object from the room, or an image of something you have witnessed. Know also that anytime you can return to the magic room for comfort or further revelations. You have the key.

Opening a Soda Can

Knowing When to Keep a Secret

*W*hat happens when you open a soda bottle or can? There's a pop, a hiss, as the soda starts to lose its fizz. All the effervescence that was contained in the sealed system now commences to dissipate into the atmosphere. The unsealed soda grows flat.

People are much the same. Ever see someone almost visibly lose their bubbles? They have a wonderful idea or project and in the first flush of enthusiasm rush to share it with another. The listener is a bit more blasé. "That's a good idea, but…" Or, "That reminds me of something I read about…" Or even worse, "Yes, but here's how you could do it even better." Pretty soon the fizz is gone; original enthusiasm has lessened; the genie has fled the uncorked lamp.

It's not that you always have to be secretive. Nothing wrong with opening a soda and pouring some out for others. But if the drinks are poured before your guests are ready to drink them, the soda goes flat, the ice melts—the results are disappointing.

So consider this principle when something bubbles in your soul. A God-experience. A fresh idea. A new mantra you are working with. A new direction for your life. A moment of beauty when you are walking in the woods or brushed on the cheek by a poem. There's a temptation to pigeonhole someone immediately and share it all. But ask yourself, is this the right time, place, and person?

And what's your motive—to pass on to others gifts received? To grow closer with loved ones? Or to turn that precious moment into a memento? To capture it like a butterfly and pin it down with words?

Are you taking an experience freely given you and trying to sell it? Or to sell yourself by showcasing your special sensitivities? If so, might it be better, at least for now, to keep quiet?

In a society loopy for info exchange—fax, e-mail, Internet, and eighty channels on cable—it can seem a moral duty to blurt out everything. But sometimes what's good for soda is good for the soul: keeping it shut up and fizzy.

Is there anything you need to keep shut up for now (or, conversely, to pop open because the moment is right)?

Shaving With a Razor
The Merits of a Daily Practice

*A*ny man or woman who shaves knows this truth: the hairs grow back. It doesn't matter what a nice, close shave you have accomplished. Immediately the hair begins to grow, and soon forms a stubble, calling for another shave. To shave once and expect it to suffice indefinitely is clearly to misunderstand the process. A once a year tune-up might work for a car depending upon how often it is driven. But the biological growth of hair is constant, and so in need of constant remedy.

Such it is with a hairy mind. The Buddhists speak of *tanha*, self-centered craving, as the root of all suffering. The Judeo-Christian tradition refers to *sin*, a tendency to miss the mark that is rooted in our human nature. We seem to have an inborn propensity to sprout the "hairs" of selfishness, fear, jealousy, petty resentment, bitterness, and egotism. No matter how clean-shaven we begin the day (whether through prayer, affirmations, meditation, a nature-walk), it's fairly predictable that by midday we'll be developing the beginning of that "five-o'clock shadow" (for men), that stubble (for women) that calls for another shave. It would be foolish to abandon all shaving in frustration, claiming that it doesn't seem to work. On the contrary, because it *does* work, we need to commit ourselves to a frequent and regular practice.

What is it that gives us a good clean mental shave—that is, clears away the forming fears, stress, and resentments? Just as there are many kinds of razors, so too, cleansing practices. One person might dig in the garden. Another sits down with a good novel and a cup of tea. A third gives the problem over to a Higher Power, affirming faith that all will be well. Another looks honestly at where she's been at fault in a situation, letting go of blaming the other.

You wouldn't shave just at times of dire need. It's simply a habit, built into our daily routine. This is also the best way to use those spiritual practices. So lather up, get out the razor, and give yourself a shave.

How do you shave, mentally and spiritually speaking? Is it a regular part of your daily or weekly routine?

❖

The day of my spiritual awakening was the day I saw—and knew I saw—all things in God and God in all things.

MECHTILD OF MAGDEBURG,
MEDIEVAL CHRISTIAN MYSTIC

❖

Throwing Things Away
Creating Space and Time

*I*n the Hindu trinity of Gods there is Brahma the creator, Vishnu the preserver, and Shiva the destroyer. Without the power of Shiva, clearing out the old, there would be no space for new creation. Sometimes depicted wearing a necklace of skulls, Shiva is nonetheless a beneficent God integral to the cycle of life.

Man, it feels good to play Shiva. Ever notice how domestic life has a tendency, as firmly established as the physical law of entropy, to become more and more cluttered? At least in our *rush, stay busy, and buy* culture we are much more prone in our quest for fulfillment to acquire things than to slice them away. So we schedule in new activities for ourselves or, perhaps worse, for our kids—ballet lessons, gymnastics, trips to the mall, whatever. We purchase new items to fill unrequited needs. "I must have that new sound system with the six interlocked play-modules." Gifts pour in, especially on designated holy days, as if this new ceramic mug or that salad spinner would really make us whole. More likely all this stuff will soon make us crazy if it continues to pile up.

Thank God for Shiva! Yes, how good it feels, how divine, to clear out room amidst the rubbish. Whenever we throw something away we also create something of value—nothing less than *space* and *time*. Give away those clothes I haven't worn in years—I've created more space in the closet. Cancel those gymnastics lessons—I've created more time for the family to lounge about, enjoying sabbath leisure.

Rereading the Genesis story we find that God was not just creating things. He was also throwing stuff away, or at least straightening up, so as to make space for the new. ("And God said, 'Let the waters under the sky be gathered together into one place, and let the dry land appear.'") You can imagine the Omnipotent One adding, "There, that's much better, everything in its proper place. Now I can sit in peace and enjoy a cup of tea." ("And he rested on the seventh day.")

So when we get rid of unnecessary stuff that is threatening to engulf us—and when we straighten up that which remains—let us think of this as a Godly task. Toss away that ornamental plate that no one likes. Bag those old toys and give them to someone who might use them. Clear off those desk surfaces that never see the light of day. Let there be light. Yes, you have embarked on a holy mission: creating *holes* in a cluttered world.

What in your life (material objects, excess activities, outworn commitments) needs to be thrown away or radically reorganized? Might you make a small start on that today?

Recycling Garbage
Using the Trash of Our Life

*G*arbage cans are filled with the detritus of civilization. Poke around in one and you might find banana peels, empty soda bottles, the remnants of a frozen TV dinner, a crushed appliance box, coffee grounds, and on and on, all mixed together in a crazy heap waiting to be carted away. To call it "garbage" is to declare we've no further use for it. We have taken what we wish for our pleasure and sustenance and discarded the remains. As with the remains of a person, they are ready to be interred or burnt to a crisp.

If a city produces too much garbage it can soon be overwhelmed. We are surrounded by landfills, and air and water grown toxic from our refuse and its disposal. The same can become true of our life. We may deem so much of it garbage: a failing relationship; an irritating boss; aspects of our body and personality we could gladly do without (fat thighs, frizzy hair, a nasty temper). We'd love to toss these things away. When that proves impossible, we're left living in trash.

Of course, one person's garbage is another's wealth. Notice a homeless person picking through trash cans, seeking bottles to be turned in for cash. Or watch a stray cat outside a Chinese restaurant, rooting about for delicious morsels. A sculptor finds metal scraps in a junkyard. A gardener looks at rotten banana peels and sees valuable mulch.

Each is a form of recycling, the discovery of that which can be salvaged and re-used. So too can we recycle our personal garbage. It's only "refuse" as long as we refuse it.

A dying relationship? Perhaps we need to reclaim what first brought us together, and renew our commitment and love. Even if this proves impossible, there may be something valuable to gain from the "failure." It may teach us to choose the next partner more carefully, or to work on our emotional blocks. We're laying down mulch for the next relationship in hope that it will bear more fruit.

A nasty boss: how to recycle that? Maybe we'll finally learn to stand up for ourselves. Conversely, this could be the perfect opportunity to develop more patience and tact. Or perhaps it's a sign from the universe that the time has come to pursue another job, one better suited to our talents.

There's no rulebook here. While dumping garbage is a crude affair, recycling is an art. Hand a kid an empty appliance box on a rainy Sunday and you're likely to see it put to a dozen different uses. As adults we become far more reductive: It's an empty box, for god's sake throw it out!

But once committed to recycling, we can reclaim that suppleness of mind. We may even get radical and decide there's no such thing as garbage, that every mess has its uses and lessons if we work with it creatively. As important as recycling is for the planet, so it is for our quality of life.

What "garbage" in your life needs to be creatively recycled? What might this mean—how can you salvage, learn from, use even that which you now count as trash?

The Baal-Shem teaches that no encounter with a being or a thing in the course of our life lacks a hidden significance. The people we live with or meet with, the animals that help us with our farm work, the soil we till, the materials we shape, the tools we use, they all contain a mysterious spiritual substance which depends on us for helping it towards its pure form, its perfection.

MARTIN BUBER,
*THE WAY OF MAN ACCORDING
TO THE TEACHINGS OF HASIDISM*

Uncapping a Fire Hydrant
Releasing Hidden Resources

I grew up in a busy city—New York, to be precise. On nearly every street squatted a fire hydrant blending into the urban landscape. An occasional dog did his duty there. Now and again, in the hot summer months, a hydrant might be uncorked to release a cooling shower for sweaty kids. But for the most part the hydrant rested unobtrusive, unwanted, and unrecognized.

Except at times of emergency. If, God forbid, a fire broke out, the hydrant came into its own. It stepped onto the scene as life-saver, able to direct a surge of water with astounding force to quench the raging holocaust. Like Superman casting off his Clark Kent glasses, the hydrant revealed hidden POWER.

We may surprise ourselves one day by doing the same. In our ordinary lives we all too often are selfish, petty, and distracted. We may dimly sense the seeds of greatness within but rarely live up to this promise. We're just people, after all, limited and flawed. Or so we think.

But imagine a Clark Kent who has forgotten his true identity. One morning, witnessing a crime or natural disaster, a strange urge he doesn't fully understand leads him to locate a phone booth (remember those?) and strip. Weird. But underneath his street clothes, to his astonishment, he finds a Superman cape—*and then he remembers*.

Sometimes we are like that, surprising to ourselves. A child of ours falls ill and we sit up through the long night conquering exhaustion to respond lovingly to her need. Or a flood descends on our town washing lives away. For a solid week we participate in relief efforts, at great inconvenience, but without complaint. That's not like us, this level of generosity. Or we hear of a friend with a cancer diagnosis. The compassion we offer, the strength and wisdom we access, feels as if derived from a Higher Power.

Maybe we're like that fire hydrant. The hydrant, after all, is not the source of the waters that flow through its body. This stub of metal is too small to contain them. But the hydrant can chan-nel a torrent. All that's needed is to remove the cap that keeps the waters in check. This we do when the situation demands and when in our heart we consent.

Our methods for uncapping the hydrant vary. One person squares her shoulders to face head-on what is to come. Another falls to his knees, knowing he needs help. A third remembers kind-nesses received over the years and is inspired to follow suit. A fourth feels the call of duty and responds. One way or another we uncap the hydrant—and the waters begin to flow.

Later on, if there's time for reflection, we may ask ourselves, "Where did that energy come from? How did I know to say what I did? How did I accomplish that much when ordinarily I'm so limited? Who am I after all? What is my true self?"

Good questions. What, after all, is that fire hydrant—a small metal stump, or the conduit for a mighty river? Depends on whether it's uncapped.

When is the last time you uncapped the hydrant and felt a surprising outflow of wisdom, energy, or love? How might you do that more, without needing a crisis to provoke it? That is, what methods help you unplug the hydrant?

Stillness and Motion

Can you wait quietly until the mud settles,
the way becomes clear?
Can you remain still
until the moment of action?

TAO TE CHING, #15

Still Things

Learning to Be, Not Just Do

*H*ave you ever noticed how inanimate objects rest, for the most part, absolutely still? Look around your kitchen. The dishes are just where you left them (darn it!) piled up in the sink. The utensils wait patiently in their cubbyholes until you spring them into action. The wallpaper still clings to the wall (for the most part). It's *still there* because it is *still*.

Regard these objects as spiritual teachers. Don't they provide a crucial object lesson, especially in our rush-rush world? For to be still is one of the hardest, yet most necessary things for a person to do. Or *to be*, we should say, for the concept of "doing" implies action, movement, change. Finally, we are human beings, not just human doings. We flourish best when our life is seeded with a generous amount of being still. Call it Sabbath-mind, one-pointed attention, the emptiness that allows God to fill us up. All sacred traditions honor the stillness however they choose to name it.

Think of the last time you noticed the beauty of nature—clouds gliding overhead, or the murmurings of a stream—wasn't it because you had grown still? Or the last time you had a powerful experience of prayer, or insight, or reverence. Wasn't it because you had become quiet enough to hear an inner voice or to gaze upon the mysteries that surround you?

Always in motion, we are like cameras whose snapshots necessarily blur. We rush through work, conversations, and meals as if there were no tomorrow. The truth is that in such a state there is *no today*. What did I have for lunch? What were you saying about your sister? Everything speeds by slightly out of focus.

The better photograph is taken by a camera held still. Similarly, the mind works better when held still. For once, don't just do something, sit there. But that's so hard to do and to be!

So give thanks that we are surrounded by inanimate Buddhas willing to teach us how to slow down. That pair of pants draped over the chair. Those keys, resting inert, on the mantelpiece. The bed on which you fling your tired body. The reading lamp, neck bent, as if in prayer. Each has nowhere to go. Nothing to do. Each rests quiet, empty, still.

Try spending a little time today with one still thing of your choosing. Watch it do nothing, just be what it is. Try to get a feel for it in your own body. View it as your teacher. Can you absorb a bit of its patience and tranquility?

❖

Nothing in all creation is so like God as stillness.

MEISTER ECKHART,
MEDIEVAL CHRISTIAN MYSTIC

❖

SHAPE-SHIFT
Pretend You Are Your Own Clothes

BENEFITS: stillness, relaxation, a letting-go of the ego's agenda

Lie down on your bed or a comfortable couch. Take a few minutes to breathe deeply, allowing your mind and body to relax. Now imagine that, for a few minutes, instead of being yourself you are your own clothes. This might be the clothing you are in right now as you meditate. For example, if you are lying in bed wearing a shirt and sweatpants, pretend the scene is just as it is except *there's no you there*: just your shirt and sweats laid out on the bed. (Or you imagine a different outfit lying on the bed, perhaps your favorite, or most comfortable.)

Feel the delightful sense of being totally still—clothes, of course, cannot move, but lie wherever they've been left. Feel a wonderful vacancy—clothes are not afflicted with a busy mind, or any mind at all. Imagine that gravity is gradually smoothing out your wrinkles. This will help you release any physical tightness or knots. If you wish, imagine that your breathing is the steam heat of a laundry—it circulates through your body, cleaning you and smoothing you out. Aaah, it feels good just to let go thoroughly, nowhere to go, nothing to do until your owner returns.

Beds
Rest and Support

*B*eds are, first and foremost, the place where we rest. Oh, I know other, more active, things that people can do in bed. But such couplings are possible only because the bed opens a space where we may rest with another, or *on* another, exploring each other in leisured intimacy.

Rest is the guiding principle, the *raison d'être* of a bed. That's why the bed is such a vivid (if often overlooked) symbol of the spiritual life. Why do we turn to God? Why do millions the world over pray, meditate, chant? Isn't it because we all simply want some rest—from the clamors of the world, the doubt and confusion that tear the soul, the suffering that plagues even the most blessed life, and the seemingly ceaseless mental chatter? The great prayer of the ages is—"Dear Lord, give me rest!" (Advanced seekers add, "And help others rest too!")

The bed, like God, grants rest. It is always available, day and night, for a good lie-down. It opens the doors to the realm of sleep, that miraculous kingdom which heals and restores without us having to do anything but let go.

The bed allows sleep because it is *lower* than our body. By humbly taking upon itself our weight, it relieves us of our daily battle with gravity. We often think of God as a Lord on high commanding from the heavens. But the Tao te Ching portrays the Divine as lowly:

> All streams flow to the sea
> because it is lower than they are.
> Humility gives it its power. (#66)

The Divine sustains us from beneath. Like the sea, yes, but also like a bed: firm enough to support our burdens yet soft enough to grant rest.

And we can form such a bed for one another. Someone approaches you to share their troubles—a difficult child, a stressful work situation, a suspicious spot on a mammogram. The temptation is to turn into something helpful. Let me be a telephone hotline offering referrals, or a doctor's kit filled with remedies. But instead why not just be a bed? That is, assume the humble posture of simply *being there*. Allow your friend, in speaking, to put down the burden; to sit on the edge of your listening ear; to slip off tight shoes; and finally to lie down, as you support her, gently yet reliably. Be a bed and furnish its blessings.

Which people in your life are like a bed for you when you need that support? At some time today can you lie down in a bed (literal or metaphorical) to rest? Can you also to take a few minutes to be a bed for another person?

Crutches

Learning to Lean

*O*ne accusation directed toward religiously minded people is that they use their faith as a crutch. In a society that values self-reliance this is a damning image indeed. It implies that you cannot stand upright on your own. Weak and unsteady, you need outside support. To rely on a crutch is to be a cripple, insufficient to cope with life's pressures.

Yes, that's right. But what's wrong with that? A crutch is a source of strength, support, and equilibrium, a power we can lean on. Something that completes what is missing, helps to make us whole. What better description is there of a Higher Power? What better aid on our journey through life?

It's nice to fantasize that we need no such crutch. The ego-self would prefer to be thoroughly in charge but time and again proves insufficient to the task. On our own we stumble into poor decisions, tense relations, and painful emotions. We grow exhausted by the challenges of the day. The slings and arrows of outrageous fortune—disappointments, illness, broken loves, and even the pressures of unexpected success—can overwhelm our precarious balance until we're ready to topple over in a breeze. Help!

Introduce the crutch, and equilibrium returns. Prayer strengthens us in a moment of despair. A meditative pause gives rise to guidance where once confusion reigned. Out of kilter, we repeat a holy name and it helps us to calm and center. Yes, it's all a crutch, but what's wrong with that? This cripple can walk again.

Over time the more we employ a crutch, the less it seems external to the self. The body grows so used to it that it becomes as if part of the body, incorporated seamlessly into our movement. And so, too, with God, and the devices whereby we access this Power. With faithful practice, they become part of us. "I am healed!" shouts the cripple as he throws away his crutch. In truth this is because he and the crutch are now one—the healing power has come within.

What crutch do you lean on when in need of help? Do you remember to reach for it before taking a nasty fall?

Steps, Stairs, and Escalators
The Spiritual Climb

"Step" is a funny word. It's something a body can do—as when you take a step backward, or upward. It's also something a mind, or really a whole person, can do—as when we say someone has "taken a step forward" in his life by entering a new relationship or job. A "step" is also a feature of the outside world. We speak of stairs as being composed of steps—that is, small, separate platforms to be climbed one by one. Steps—physical, existential, environmental—what, finally, are they?

As a first step to understanding, imagine climbing a stairway. You begin at the bottom gazing toward a distant goal. How to get from the first to the second floor? Unaided, your body would be stymied. It can neither float nor fly. The distance between here and there is too great, too vertical, given the downward pull of gravity. You seem irremediably earthbound.

But the stairway changes everything. Now you have a path your body can traverse. In fact, the path and body are a perfect fit, like a glove is to a hand. In walking you thrust out one foot while stabilizing balance with the other; the stairway allows you to convert this movement into purposeful climbing, a little forward, a little upward, step by step, until—voila!—you have ascended a whole floor.

The spiritual life is little different. By nature we are not angelic beings, but firmly rooted to the earth. Whatever heights we wish to reach, we're unlikely to soar there in a paroxysm of ecstasy or by serenely floating above life's conflicts. No, we climb step by step, a bit forward, a bit upward, our movement barely discernible. A prayer here. An honest talk there. A little meditation. A mumbled confession. We might doubt we are making any spiritual progress at all yet, peering over the side, the view comes to look a bit different. We have a slightly broader perspective on life, a little more distance from the problems that so weighed us down.

The notion of progress via steps is central to the "Twelve Step" program used in Alcoholics Anonymous and other such fellowships. It seems an impossible journey to get from being a drunk, life lying in ruins, to being a sober, joyful, and respected member of the community. "Don't worry," says the AA sponsor to the newcomer. "You don't have to become a saint overnight. Just take it one step at a time and you'll be amazed at the changes that will come."

There are the steps of a stairway but also, in the modern world, the steps of an escalator. Plant your feet, relax, hold onto the rail, and the moving stairs do the rest. Sometimes, happy to say, the spiritual journey works like this. Call it grace—the intercession of the Holy Spirit—the Intuitive Self at work (or at play)—when a Power transports us aloft. A song comes on the radio and provides the message we need to hear. Just as our own energy gives out, friends unexpectedly gather to lift our burdens. Or we feel consoled and illuminated by a mysterious Presence as real as it is undefinable. Suddenly, progress is rapid. We're on a spiritual escalator—just surrender and enjoy the ride.

But sooner or later (usually sooner) we're likely to find that escalator out of order. God does not do all the work for us, thank God. Our muscles would atrophy, our spirit grow lazy, if we never had to climb any steps.

What steps have you taken lately on your spiritual journey? (Count even the small ones.) Are you stuck on a landing or trudging forward, step by step, on your climb?

Magnets

The Force of Spiritual Alignment

*D*o you know how a piece of iron becomes magnetized? The potential is always there because an iron atom contains spinning electrons that create a magnetic field. Left to themselves, iron atoms are mini-magnets, but they point randomly hither and yon, effectively canceling each other out. Yet when a bar magnet is placed near a piece of iron it lines up these atoms. Now their north poles all face in one direction, their south poles, the other. A nearby magnet has polarized the iron into another magnet.

Nature offers many examples of this sort of sympathetic resonance. Strike a tuning fork and an adjacent piece of metal will pick up the same frequency of vibration. They begin to sing in unison. This happens, as well, on the human level. Place an agitated child in the arms of a calm mother, and the child soon quiets down (or vice-versa). For good or ill, we resonate with those around us.

This is particularly evident in the case of a "magnetic" personality. Such people draw attention to themselves, as a magnet pulls iron filings around it. But even more so, they are deemed "magnetic" because of their ability to magnetize others. A dynamic CEO can get the corporation humming, everyone working in sync. Where before employee energies were pointing with random, even opposing, polarities, effectively canceling one another out, now everyone points north together. So, too, a teacher who galvanizes a class; a leader, like Gandhi, who gathers a nation; a great artist who can communicate to millions a new perception of the world.

This power is at play in our spiritual guides. What is a saint or prophet but a soul-magnet able to magnetize others? They have aligned with the Great Magnet which holds together the universe, call it Allah, or Shiva, or God. The compassion and insight of the saint then calls forth much the same in disciples.

The disorganized impulses of the disciple—generous at one moment, selfish the next—begin to unify like electrons spinning in the same direction. So, too, does the community of disciples, joining together in harmony. Thus does the life of the Spirit spread: magnets magnetizing magnets.

Which people, in your life, have served as human magnets, aligning you with your better self? (You might think of friends or relatives, mentors, teachers, public figures, authors, religious leaders.) You might choose one, and ask how you could align yourself even more with their magnetic influence.

Flags

The Wind Made Visible

A flag rippling in the wind is a beautiful thing. Not because of the flag itself. Flags often have simple designs that, while vibrant, are hardly great works of art. The artwork lies more in the undulating rhythms of form and color created by the breeze. The flag becomes incorporated in a Spanish dance whose every moment surprises. All the flag must do (and this is its nature) is remain open to the wind, dance to its tune, no hesitation.

How wonderful when we are like that flag. This experience can come in various moments and contexts. A writer follows her muse, hears the words within, and writes with ease and grace. No struggle. A dancer is taken over by the music until it dances him. A meditator follows the rising and falling of breath until she *is* the breath, diving down to a secret place, and exhaled into the limitless world. Someone praying finally gives up imploring God, multiplying words upon petitionary words. Then a quiet descends. He sits and listens . . . and hears a voice whispering within. The actions that follow express the leadings of Spirit like a flag blown about in the wind.

The world of nature teaches us this grace. A flower opens to the sun. A tree reaches upward toward the light. The ocean extends its tidal arms toward the moon and, fickle lover, collapses into the embrace of earth's gravity. It's all like a flag whipping up in the wind, responsive to surrounding forces.

The great sages, too, are blown by the wind of Spirit. As we cannot directly see wind—transparent, invisible—so we cannot directly see God. But we can witness God in the movements of a human heart, divinely inspired. Those who meet a Buddha, Jesus, or Muhammad experience the Spirit at play. They are like flags blown hither and yon by a holy wind, making it visible. So often we salute *our* flag versus *yours*, leading to dissension. How much better to celebrate the Wind that blows them all.

Today, see if you can't, even to some small degree, make yourself a flag blowing in the wind; quiet, open, receptive, surrendered.

❖

When nothing is done, nothing is left undone.
True mastery is allowing things to take their course
Without interference.

TAO TE CHING, #48

❖

Sailboats

Blown by the Spiritual Breezes

*I*magine yourself a sailboat. Not the pilot of the sailboat, skilled though she may be, but the sailboat itself, on its windblown journey.

You are solid. You must keep body and soul together even when buffeted by the wind and crashing seas. You do not have the luxury of fragility that is open to land-loving things.

At the same time your solidity must be wedded to a lightness and buoyancy that allows you to crest the waves. No heaviness here to drive you under. You must be light-hearted like a child skipping down the street, free of the adult cares that cause the older step to grow slow and ponderous.

Most of all, you must be receptive. Not even your lightness can drive you forward one whit, nor your solidity. You simply receive the wind's blessing. It takes you by the hand, now leads you forward like a comforting companion, now pulls you along like an overeager child. It would have you go this way and that, reversing directions unexpectedly, then strangely it grows becalmed. Do not seek to understand the wind's ways. It is a mystery to itself as much as to you. It is nothing other than self-discovery, born anew each moment in airy form.

So you cannot predict it. You cannot control it. All you can do is receive. This is what your sails were made for—to delight in the call of the breezes. To do so, your sails must be strong and flexible. Not fragile, ripped apart by an energetic gust, nor stiff and unyielding. They must flow with the wind until they are like wind itself, billowing and ripply.

When the winds of change blow through our life, or the winds of Spirit inspire us, there is nothing better to be than a sailboat. We must unfurl the canvas of the heart. We must not let that wind pass by, but *quick*—catch it, ride lightly in the breeze, go with the flow, and let it lead us across uncharted seas to that distant shore—our home.

At times we might rather be a motorboat. How nice to resolutely set your own course and feel powered from within. No threat of being blown hither and yon, or left to the mercy of still air. But motorboats are a mixed blessing. They can be noisy, hazardous to nearby creatures, gas-guzzlers, and prone to breakdown. So are we when we rev up the engine and motor our way through life.

So better to be a sailboat—a soul-boat. The soul was meant to be a sail trusting to the godly breeze.

In different areas of your life are you more a sailboat or a motorboat? What practices of the heart would help you unfurl your soul-sail?

SHAPE-SHIFT
Pretend You Are a Sailboat

BENEFITS: a sense of relaxation, ease, letting go of control

Imagine that you are a sailboat drifting along on the open sea. (To begin, you may wish to visualize yourself unmooring from the dock, gliding out through an inlet, and then into the open waters. Thus you gradually loosen your ties to your former location and thought patterns.) In this visualization, there is no one manning the sailboat. No self. No ego. The sailboat just drifts along, responsive to current and wind.

Imagine that your breath is that wind. You feel it fill up your body in the way a sea breeze gently billows a canvas sail. Attend to your breath with the sensitivity that a sail must feel for the wind. At times, your breath will gust a little more heavily, while at other times it will be becalmed. No matter. The sailboat has nowhere to go. No preferences. No one at the rudder. See yourself, feel yourself, drifting aimlessly, responsive only to the breath.

You may also experiment with feeling the breath as the sea's gentle waves. As the breath rises, crests, and falls, feel yourself bobbing gently on top of it, a boat riding the swells.

When thoughts come, remind yourself that there's no one on board to do the thinking. You might imagine the thoughts as seabirds circling the boat and squawking overhead. But there's no one on board to feed them. Simply return to imagining that unmanned sailboat, drifting on wind and sea.

In-Sight: Looking Deeply Into Things

Perhaps we are here to say: house,
bridge, fountain, gate, pitcher, fruit-tree, window—
or at most: column, tower. . . . But to say them,
you understand, to say them *more intensely* than
the things themselves know themselves to be.

RAINER MARIA RILKE,
NINTH DUINO ELEGY

We must learn to penetrate
things and find God there.

MEISTER ECKHART,
MEDIEVAL CHRISTIAN MYSTIC

Stained Glass
Illuminating the Universe

Why is stained glass a potent image of the divine? Not simply for its shimmering play of colors. That can be found elsewhere, for example in a neon sign. Is it because of the religious subjects stained glass windows portray? But such are present as well in paintings. There remains something unique about stained glass—its ability to elevate and illuminate—that renders it almost a cliché for the sacred.

Perhaps the key lies in examining how stained glass works. It is a transmitter, not originator, of light. Wander a church at night and the most gorgeous stained glass is reduced to a dreary shadow. Come back during the day to find it brilliantly resurrected by the sunlight streaming through. And if light brings the glass to life, the reverse is also true. Stained glass renders vivid and colorful the sunlight. Like a magician pulling colored scarves from a hat, the glass pulls forth dazzling blues, greens, and reds.

Scientists reveal how the magician performs this trick. White light combines all the wavelengths of the visible spectrum. A colored window, say one that looks yellow, actually absorbs blue light (the color complement of yellow). The rest of the spectrum passes on through to register as yellow in your eye. It's the magic of selective filtering.

Similarly, the shape of a stained glass window brings forth certain forms through excluding others. A triangular window lets through a triangle of light. A window shaped like a martyred saint creates that image for the eye. Amorphous sunlight is carved into figures.

How like the Genesis account of creation! God takes a formless void, says "Let there be light," and proceeds to divide up the world. Light is separated from dark, sky from water, and water from earth. So stained glass divides light into form and color, creating a small universe.

In the greater universe of which we are a part, we all shine like stained glass windows. Our precious qualities, the theologians say, did not originate simply within. Just as stained glass derives its glory from the sun, so are we all emanations of the One—call it God, Buddha Nature, the Tao. There is a light that floods throughout creation, energizing and illuminating all beings.

As individuals we stain that light with specificity. There is no one else who caresses my daughter's cheek just as I do. No one else with precisely your sense of humor, or way of moving through a room. These marvelous things come to be when the light shines through you and me. We, then, are crucial in God's self-expression, as are each of the other six billion human windows. We should grieve when any one is shattered.

And why stop at human beings, and not the cardinal outside my window, the blooming chestnut, the dance of clouds over-head? Each, too, is marvelous stained glass, brightening the world with its colors.

We didn't have to have this stained glass universe. The One might have stayed simply Unitary—White, Undifferentiated, All in All. But wouldn't that be boring?

Today, pause to appreciate some of the stained glass win-dows, human or otherwise, that you encounter. Try to feel a bit of the awe that a devout believer might experience when worshiping in a stained glass cathedral.

Mirrors

Reflections on Our Oneness

Mirrors, at first glance, are absurd. Like a village idiot, they are good at mimicking but not at understanding what they imitate. Whatever I do the image in the mirror does back, a comical, superficial mime. No wonder children like to clown before a mirror—the mirror is itself a clown.

But look again. Look deeper, behind the surface play of images, to find a deeper meaning to the mirror. A mirror enables me to climb outside of myself, to view myself as others do. I witness my face staring back at me as if it were that of another person. We are twinned, and I'm not even sure who I am—looker or looked at—we are so intertwined.

Look even deeper, and the mirror has a further message: All people are mirrors reflecting one another. Who am I? I look into your eyes to find there my image. Do you think me attractive, courageous, and smart, or somehow deficient? I am reflected back to myself through your gaze, as well as that of countless others I meet. And I do the same for you. I act as your mirror to show you who you are. Six billion people are six billion mirrors, reflecting one another in the funhouse of the world.

This suggests an even deeper truth: that you and I are one. Somehow we are intimately connected, as I am to my own face in the mirror. To this end tend most mystical and moral teachings such as: "Do unto others as you would have them do unto you." Instead of the "golden rule" we might call this the "mirror rule." It says treat the other person as if it were you, mirrored back in the eyes of another.

We misuse a mirror when we search in it mainly for signs of our uniqueness. "Mirror, mirror, on the wall, who's the fairest of them all?" This is to ask the mirror a surface question, and identify self with its most surface attribute. No wonder this question is attributed in *Snow White* to the wicked queen. It is a divisive question that leads to violence toward self and others. Instead, let us ask the deeper question, and hear a deep reply: "Mirror, mirror, on the wall, who am I?" "You are one with All."

Today look into the face of another and, looking beyond the surface differences, see a reflection of yourself.

We can learn to look at something and see more than an ordinary object. With the eyes of faith we can begin now to discover the holiness, the sign, hidden in each common thing, the reality and love of God all around us, by deciding to look for it.

SUE MONK KIDD,
GOD'S JOYFUL SURPRISE

Contact Lenses
Clearing Our Spiritual Vision

I wear contact lenses. Without them I'd be virtually blind (glasses cannot correct my condition). The world I inhabit would be a blur, an array of indistinct objects. Thank God for contacts. I am lucky to live in a time when the technology exists to help with my corneal malformation.

But there are other kinds of malformed vision even harder to correct. When we see through the eyes of greed we notice profits more than people. Human beings, and the humane parts of self, fade into a blurry background while gold shines bright. The eye of lust sees hot bodies but not the persons who inhabit them. The seven deadly sins are like seven astigmatisms, each distorting our vision of the world.

A spiritual insight is like inserting contact lenses. For it to make a difference we must have *contact* with it, not just gaze at it from outside. It's easy to admire the principles of a self-help book but do little to apply them. This does about as much good as a contact lens held at arm's length. No, we must slip the lens in. It must become as if a part of the eye, something we don't see as an object, but *see through*. Then a tiny bit of plastic changes the way the world appears. So, too, at the right moment a small insight, a line of scripture, a few words from a friend—well inserted— radically clarifies our view.

Of course, it's not a simple matter to have true *in-sight:* to take something in so deeply that it transforms the way we see. At first, a new contact may sit uncomfortably on the eye (especially the sort of hard lenses I wear). So too, a new way of seeing the world—as through the eyes of gratitude or compassion—takes a while to sink in. But over time these principles become part of us. Everywhere we start to see occasions for thankfulness, and people deserving of compassion, not censure.

Perhaps it's time to re-envision God. We're used to thinking of the divine as a Person or Force. But this can place God somewhere "out there," a Being hard to reach. What if God is more like a contact lens? Then the Divine is to be found within the I. It is not an object to be seen so much as that through which we see when gazing with the eyes of love. Then our astigmatism is removed. We can navigate the world reliably. "I once was lost but now am found, was blind but now can see."

Try imagining that you are inserting God into your I (eye), and for a few minutes see what the world might look like through God-eyes. What do you notice that you might otherwise have missed?

Cups

Beyond the Half-Empty and Half-Full

"You can see the cup as half-empty or half-full"—so goes the old cliché. But perhaps the cliché doesn't go far enough. To see the cup as half-empty is to focus on what's missing from our life. A stimulating job, supportive wife, respectful kids, whatever. Our attention is not so much focused on what exists but what doesn't and should, in our estimation. The good fades away to insignificance, like the Cheshire cat in *Alice in Wonderland* leaving only its grin, or in this case, its grimace. So "to see the cup as half-empty" is really to see it as *all* empty, no halfway about it. And there's nothing halfway about "seeing the cup as half-full." At such times we think about what we *do* have in our life: food on the table, say, or reasonably good health, loved ones, a bright spring day in the offing. Now, the focus lies on what is, not what isn't, and what is, when fully experienced, is *always enough*. How could it not be when we've stopped comparing reality with imaginary constructs?

> Be fulfilled in what you have,
> content with the way of things.
> When you realize nothing is lacking
> the whole world belongs to you.

(TAO TE CHING, #44)

This "seeing the cup as half-full" is really to experience it as *all* full and beyond. In the words of the Psalmist, "My cup runneth over."

Take a walk in the forest and absorb the call of a thrush; the scent of pine needles and their flowing dance in the breeze; the rhythm of your own stride and the ache of your muscles; the salty taste of your morsel of bread and cheese; the crumb carried off by a single-minded ant. You can't capture adequately singular moments in words. You can't reason them through, give them market values, or preserve them intact for tomorrow. To say "my cup runneth over" is finally to say there is no cup, no container, that can possibly hold the *real*—just the joyful pouring, ever-renewed, of life's effervescent liquid.

Try to pause some time today, or several times, to experience and celebrate the moment. Feel your cup runneth over with the real.

Guns

The Distorted Voice of the Soul

*L*et's look closely at a gun, or better yet, listen. For a gun is first and foremost a voice. It speaks *LOUDLY*. I refer not only to its ear-splitting bang, but to the powerful effects of its bullets. They can smash through barriers, tear apart a room, shred a human body, terminate a life. When a gun speaks, everyone listens. It screams out for attention: Ignore me at your peril!

Herein lies much of the attraction a gun holds for those who feel otherwise voiceless. The kid ignored in high school. The young tough roaming inner city streets. The child of squalor and perpetual war who dreams of bearing arms against the enemy. The depressed man sitting alone in a room who picks up a gun, puts it in his mouth, wondering whether to pull the trigger. Have a gun—then someone will listen. The world will take note.

In the face of all the shootings, all the tragedies, we speak of the need for gun control. This is absolutely crucial, but also insufficient. We must not only *control* guns but also find something to take their place. Thomas Moore writes in *Care of the Soul,* "In the strength of its emotions, the soul is a gun, full of potential power and effect. . . . If violence is the repressed life force showing itself symptomatically, the cure for violence is care of the soul's power. It is foolish to deny signs of this power—individuality, eccentricity, self-expression, passion—because it cannot be truly repressed."

The soul's power can speak through many voices. Write a poem. Sing. Organize a protest. Make love. Cast a vote. Buy a home. Work a job that challenges and stimulates. Cry when you need to. Dress wildly. There are a thousand voices more individual, powerful, and nuanced, than that of a gunshot. But we are often better at distributing guns (there are one hundred million in America), than supporting creative voices.

Turn around the word "evil" and you'll find the word "live." Hidden deep within the barrel of a gun there is yet that of God.

The best way to quiet the voice of death is to replace it with the myriad voices of life. May they sing forth throughout our land.

Look within at your own violent tendencies. What makes you rage, even want to kill? Ask, underneath the anger, what is your soul crying out for—love, attention, security? Honor the voice of your soul so that it need not surface destructively.

Money
"Thou Visible God"

Shakespeare calls gold "Thou *visible* God" (*Timon of Athens*, Act 4, Scene 3). Karl Marx quotes this passage in his own indictment of capitalism and its money-worship. Money, he writes, is granted a godlike power overwhelming more humane values. Of course Jesus said something like this (but with a spiritual accent) close to two thousand years before. He challenges his followers to choose between God and mammon (money)—you simply can't serve both masters. Spirituality or materialism—two worldviews, two sets of priorities, ever opposed. To worship the golden calf is to forsake the living God.

That is, unless we realize God hidden in the gold. As the words are similar—God and gold—so, too, the yearnings for each. What do we truly want when we pile up riches? Security. Freedom from want and fear. Joyful experiences. Success. The fulfillment of all our desires. But this, mystics tell us, can only be received as a gift of Spirit. Through the Divine we are truly filled full.

Our soul longs for the spiritual riches hidden in the depths of the heart. Our earthly self grasps for a tangible metaphor: It seeks gold, that precious metal hidden in the depths of the earth. The greed with which men pursue riches is like the passion which drives sincere spiritual aspirants—a willingness to give all, even one's very life, in pursuit of the Ultimate Goal.

Thus money, that most materialistic of things, turns out to be the most metaphorical—a stand-in for something else. By itself, gold is just a hunk of metal, and our current money, a bunch of paper, valueless in itself, simply a medium of exchange. The world is filled with unhappy millionaires seeking yet more money as if that would be the answer. But when we realize the symbol as symbol—gold as a symbol of spiritual wealth—it reminds us to "not store up for yourselves treasures on earth, where moth and decay destroy, and thieves break in and steal, but store up treasures in heaven" (Matthew 6:19–20).

That doesn't necessarily mean giving away all our money. It does mean looking at our money with a new eye. When you pull out a dollar bill, pay less attention to the front where it is proclaimed to be legal tender. Look instead at the message on the back, so rarely pondered: "In God we trust." Then our wallet is filled with spiritual reminders, prayer cards in the form of cash.

This may also lead us to use our money in more considered ways. That twenty-dollar bill can buy a gift for our child; a book that awakens our own mind and heart; or several meals at a shelter for the homeless. Each choice creates a slightly different world as we partner with God, a co-Creator. So let us neither worship money nor throw it away in the pursuit of unsatisfying distractions. Let us find in our gold that most precious thing—a spark of the Divine.

Take some money out of your wallet. Look at it with new eyes as a material form of Divine energies waiting to be unleashed. Think now about the different ways you might spend it.

THREE

Human Being

The Wisdom
of the Body

Wind, rain, dew, thunder, sun and moon,
stars, animals and plants, mountains and rivers,
earth and stones are essentially of one body with
human beings. It is for this reason that things like
grain and animals can nourish us, medicine and
minerals heal us. Sharing the same ch'i (material
energy) we enter into one another.

WANG YANG-MING,
NEO-CONFUCIAN PHILOSOPHER

Do not disdain your body.
For the soul is just as safe in its body
as in the kingdom of heaven.

MECHTILD OF MAGDEBURG,
MEDIEVAL CHRISTIAN MYSTIC

The Body
Lover of the World

When a human body meets a rock lying by the road, it says I know you. I know you with my eyes that scan your surface, my hands that feel your weight. But I know you even more intimately than that, for I hold you within my bones which are stone-like. They anchor me as you are anchored; they give me rigid structure like you. I know you, rock, because you are inside me.

And when the body gazes upward and sees a cloud in the sky, it says I know you, too. I see you cloud, I see you sky, and I feel the gentle breeze on my face. But I know you also because you are inside me. I breathe in the air and it aerates all my muscles and tissues making me fertile and alive. The clean air passes in and out of me, lightening my spirit. I exhale small clouds of water vapor that are carried away on the breeze.

When the body comes to the edge of the ocean it says I know you, too. My blood is salty just like yours. My life (says the body) first came from the ocean, and I still have an inner ocean, the tides and eddies of blood that wash against the shore of cells as numerous as sand. And I feel the rhythm of your waves in my heartbeat, in the flow of in-breath and out-breath, which crash and recede like waves.

And I know you, tree, says the body. I know what it is to be anchored to the earth and yet rising vertically, on a tall trunk, reaching for the heavens, arms extended. And I know you flower, says the body. I know what it feels like to turn to the sun and follow it like a lover seeking everywhere and only the face of the beloved.

Finally the body says I know you *everything*. We are friends. No, more than that, we are lovers. No, even more than that, we are One. From dust I have come, and unto dust I shall return. But not only dust—water also, and air, and mountain, and river, and sun, and rain. Everywhere I go I meet my lover, I meet myself. Let the spirit fly off to metaphysical realms if it so desires, says the body. For me, the physical is sacred enough, the earth my one true home.

Today go for a walk and feel how deeply your body is at home in the world, especially the natural world with its air, earth, and waters, its plants and creatures.

The Human Face

Each the Face of God

❖

The best picture of the human soul is the human body.

LUDWIG WITTGENSTEIN,
PHILOSOPHICAL INVESTIGATIONS

❖

Take a moment to look at someone's face, preferably when you are unobserved. (You're not as self-conscious then, freer to focus on the other.) Looking at a photo will do in a pinch, but a living face is better—your child watching TV, a friend reading the newspaper, someone at the next table caught up in conversation.

In the eyes you'll find a spark like fire—the spark of life, awareness, soul. In the curve of the mouth, the tilt of the head, emotions flow forth like water. You'll also gain a sense of all that is held within. The face presented to the outside world is but a skin covering limitless depths. We do not see all that lies beneath the surface of the sea—strange fish, undulating sea-plants, exotic caverns, and coral reefs. So, too, with a face. It's the place where the soul's ocean meets the sky, both revealing and concealing her depths.

Notice the absolute uniqueness of each face. No two are alike in all the world, in all of history. It is not just the physiognomic differences between a hooked and a snub nose, high cheekbones or a chubby grin. The true differences among faces goes deeper. They are rooted in the uniqueness of personal history and character. One face tells the story of a divorce that carved lines in the forehead and daubed the eyes with a permanent mascara of sadness. Another speaks of the greed for gold that leaves the lips pursed and grim. A twisted sense of humor, or a wide-eyed innocence, curve a face in divergent ways.

To look at faces, then, is like gazing into a series of funhouse mirrors each with its own twists and bends. We catch a glimpse in every face of the whole world mirrored back through the unique perspective of the bearer. Is it a sad world or joyful? Filled with disappointments or graces? Depends on whose face we see, and see the world through.

But not just a funhouse mirror, each face is also the stained glass through which the light of God streams. Here is divine energy present before us, uniquely expressed in this body-soul. To look deeply into another is an act of prayer. It is written in the Bible that you cannot see the face of God and live, but perhaps we come closest when we really look into another's face.

But that may screw up our plans. It certainly becomes harder to ignore, dismiss, or mistreat the other. No wonder we thrust a hood over the criminal led to execution, or turn away from the homeless woman rather than meet her eyes. It's easy to slay faceless enemies from a distance employing the video games of modern warfare. It's hard to gaze into another's eyes, then kill.

So much would change if we really looked at others we meet—our mother, our child, the store clerk, the waitress. Of course, there's a problem here, or an invitation. To look deep into another's eyes risks that they will look deeply into you. At that moment, a spark flies. God meets God. And human weakness meets weakness. Can we bear so much revelation?

Really look today into at least one person's face and see all you find there—emotion, history, desire, the spark of soul. If you dare, let this person look back at you. Alternatively, look at yourself in a mirror with this depth of gaze.

Standing

The Unity of Earth and Sky

*I*n the act of standing we unite earth and sky. Our feet are planted firmly on the ground as gravity exerts its downward pull. Yet something also calls us upward, limbs and torso and head rising, until our mind seems to inhabit the heavens. (Buddhists imagine consciousness as a clear sky through which thoughts drift like clouds before passing away.)

How to understand standing? Textbooks often portray it as the body's battle with gravity. True, it is an accomplishment which involves strenuous exertion. Over the years the upright posture takes its toll on our knees and spine, which were originally designed for a creature who walks on all fours. Fatigue sets in even in the course of a single day. We long for our allies, the chair and bed, to fight gravity on our behalf.

But this warlike image is not fair to gravity's blessings. It is our anchor to the world, keeping us grounded. Think of the astronaut floating about a weightless chamber, struggling to perform the most rudimentary functions in a chaotic and disoriented world. We might even say gravity anchors our moral life. We speak of the person of *gravity* who knows where she *stands.* Fixity of character is somehow modeled on our fixedness to the earth.

But we also speak of the need for *high* ideals, of standing *up* for beliefs, and *rising above* the petty concerns in which so many are mired. Wedded to the earth, humans also reach for the skies.

We are not alone in this. So much of nature loves up. Trees are drawn skyward by the sun's blessings, stretching branch and leaf ever higher. Giraffes grow long necks to reach high leaves. Monkeys cavort in the forest canopy, leaping from tree to tree. And on and on it goes, creatures longing to feast on the sun, to see farther, or swoop through unbounded space. It's as if gravity is countered by a natural buoyancy, an anti-gravity of body and spirit.

In harmonious standing we feel this balance of forces. We are neither sagging over like a ruined house, nor floating away like a helium balloon. Rather, we are like the tree—firmly rooted but thrusting up. We are like the mountain, with solid base and lofty peak. Our feet kiss the mother earth who gave us birth, but our head is lifted aloft. This bodily balance is expressed in our conduct. We are open to heavenly inspiration, but well-grounded in the actions we choose.

Let us then bless the upright posture. Standing up enables us to be human and to *under-stand*—stand under—the Divine.

Today, as you stand up, take a few moments to feel deeply the power of your stance, the balance of height and gravity, the freedom of movement and sight, that are present in your upright posture.

Walking
Falling With Style

Step, step, step. It's so easy to slip into the mindless rhythm of walking. The fact that walking can be so mindless is key to its charm and utility. While trudging along we can focus on other things: enjoying the weather, planning the day ahead, or worrying about minutiae. But turn attention for a moment to the walking itself and you're in for a surprise.

In *Toy Story*, the popular children's movie, Buzz Lightyear is a toy astronaut who doesn't know he's just a plaything. He tries to prove he can truly fly. A combination of slide, trampoline, and toy airplane temporarily propel Buzz aloft. He's thrilled. "That's not flying," his friend, the more sensible Woody, breaks in. "That's just falling with style." And we could say the same of walking. Upon reflection, it's just falling with style.

Try it. You push off your back foot, thrust ahead with your torso, then begin a kind of tumble forward. Your front foot saves you when it hits the ground. In a controlled fashion, you've fallen one step ahead. Then the whole business continues as your feet reverse roles, catcher becoming thruster.

What's the moral of this story? Simply this: If controlled falling is the best way to propel our bodies through life, why should it be different for our souls? We have emotional ups and downs, wild career swings, and relationship thrills and frustrations. One day we feel like a great parent, the next day befuddled by our child. Times of spiritual illumination flare up and depart, leaving us to grope in the darkness. Sometimes it feels like we're just falling, falling, falling.

Yes we are. But *we can fall with style*. Each disappointment, failed dream, and aggravation has the potential to propel us in some way forward—in humility, compassion, healthy detachment, the ability to laugh, to let go, and to love. Confronted with a difficult family member, we call on a reserve of patience we didn't even know was there. A loved one dies and we grieve, it seems forever. Then one fine spring day we surprise ourselves with a smile.

That's when we know our front foot has caught the ground and our stumble is arrested. We didn't land in the gutter after all. In fact, we're a step farther along in our journey. Time to push off again, and, guess what?—fall once more.

It would be nice to cruise through life in a smooth-gliding sports car. If I just had enough money. The right partner. The right prayer. But soon enough this proves to be a mirage: engine overheats, wheels fall off, and we're back to walking the walk, falling the fall. But at least we can fall with style.

Think of some area of your life (a relationship, job, etc.) which you might describe as a state of controlled falling. Can you see the ways in which, despite the failures, you are falling forward? What does it mean to you, in this and other areas, to fall with style?

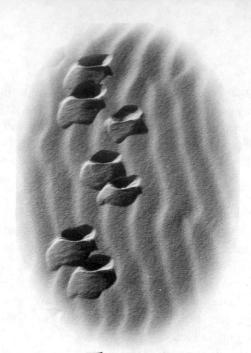

Footprints

The Presence of the Past

❖

The true miracle is not to fly in the air,
or to walk on water . . .
But to walk on this earth.

TRADITIONAL CHINESE PROVERB

❖

*W*alking down a muddy lane, or one covered with snow, what do you see? Footprints, left by sneakers and shoes, each with its own distinctive tread, or by animals treading on paw and claw. Those who came before made their mark.

This seems an ordinary thing until we reflect on it more deeply. The past has not fully passed, says the footprint—the past is *present*. It has left its impression. Just as our memories are like footprints of experiences now passed, impressed on our neurons, so the world's memories are stamped on its elemental brain.

What's more, *everything* is footprints. Not just the mark in the mud, but the mud itself: It's a memory of all the ground-up rock, the pulverized leaves, the falling rain, now congealed together. Or take the footprints in snow—isn't the snow itself a kind of footprint of yesterday's frigid winds turning moisture into intricate designs? The present is but the past preserved. And in what I do this moment I lay down a footprint for the future.

The theologians say that from God's perspective past, present, and future are one. It's all the cosmic Now. That's also true to a degree for us time-bound beings. If the *now* contains footprints of the past, and lays them down for the future, all regions of time intertwine.

To catch a glimpse of this, look at the footprints left by a traveler. You can see the walker's starting point, the steps along his journey, the destination to which he headed. For the traveler this unfolded sequentially. But we now see it, like God, all at once.

Greek philosopher Diogenes Laertius wrote, "Time is the image of eternity." Might time be eternity's footprint?

When you go outside today, look for a footprint and think of the being who left it and their journey. What footprints will you leave behind today through your thoughts, words, and actions?

Sleep
Re-connecting to the Source

*W*hat if sleep were an awakening, and our wakefulness mere dreams?

Each morning we wake up to our customary identities. One person is a movie star, another, a bum. One woman arises to find herself again the CEO of a major company, another, a housewife and mother. We resume habitual lives that we designate as *real*, so fully do we identify with these identities. But are they truly more real than who we are when asleep?

When asleep (and here I refer to deep unconscious sleep, not the halfway house of the dreaming mind) we are one with the All. The movie star, bum, CEO, housewife, relinquish the separate details of personality and circumstance that set them apart from one another. Together they lapse back into the great Void (or Plenitude) from which we all emerged prior to birth, and may return to after death.

Why is sleep so needed by living creatures, so restorative to the run-down body and mind? Why, as Shakespeare says, is it "Sleep that knits up the ravell'd sleave of care" (*Macbeth*, II, ii, 36)? Deep sleep is not just a nowhere, a nothing. It is a home to which we return for healing. A home to which we *must* regularly return, or grow weary, deteriorate, and die. Born of the Eternal, we cannot live long apart from the Source. A single day of separate life, necessarily characterized by struggles and fears, joys and anxieties, is enough to exhaust our resources. Just as an appliance needs to be recharged by an energy source, so each night we plug back into a Higher Power that our batteries may be recharged.

Scientists have not yet solved the mystery of sleep. Why is it necessary? What are its physiological mechanisms and effects? Perhaps we had best start at a different level, metaphysical more than physical. In sleep, our soul returns to the Whole. By day we inhabit an ego-world, living out the dream of prince or pauper. But at night, in dreamless sleep, we are embraced by the Beloved—re-collected into the One.

> When the mind is stilled in dreamless sleep,
> It brings rest and repose to the body.
> Just as birds fly to the tree for rest,
> All things in life find their rest in the Divine.
>
> PRASHNA UPANISHAD

Before going to sleep tonight pause to consider this a sacred act. You are placing body and soul into the hands of God, journeying back to the One.

Insomnia

The Blessing Wrapped Inside the Curse

*O*f all the frustrating syndromes that beset humanity, insomnia may be one of the worst. Trivial, yes, beside famine and pestilence. And yet to yearn for sleep and be unable to find it—to slowly, and finally, after much effort and waiting, begin to drift off, only to be jolted awake; to know that the patient struggle must begin all over again, maybe to meet the same abortion; to anticipate one's exhaustion in the day to come and yet be absolutely unable to prevent it; to know in fact that all effort is self-defeating—and thus to while away the night in loneliness, darkness, and aggravation—what a metaphor for the human spirit at its most restless and impotent. St. John writes of the dark night of the soul, but worst is when we meet this night tossing and turning, insomniac as all hell.

Yet let's look at the bright side of this darkness. At night, certain things become apparent that are hidden in the light of day. Just as the sun covers over the vastness of the starry sky, so daytime limits our perspective. It is in the long dark nights of the soul (and here St. John would agree) that certain depths are reached, certain truths revealed, that cannot be got at any other way.

Jesus in the garden of Gethsemane asks his disciples to "stay awake with me" through the agonizing night that precedes his capture. Nonetheless, they drop off to sleep. Perhaps Jesus' wish is not only for companionship, but somehow for the betterment of the disciples themselves. If they are to plumb the depths of

Spirit, including the Cross, they must learn to be insomniac, to last out those long hours from dusk to dawn, and find within them enlightenment—or, at least the truths of *endarkenment*.

So the next time you cannot sleep, look on it more as a blessing than a curse—a blessing wrapped inside the curse, like one of those hard candies with a chewy sweet center that reveals itself only when you bite really hard. Maybe God is saying "Stay awake with me. There's something to learn tonight, some shadow to confront. Maybe it's time to change your life. Maybe there's a problem that needs to be faced before you can find your repose. Maybe you're in need of inspiration. You may hear a message in the quiet of night that would be drowned out in the din of day. And finally I will give you sleep, a pillow for your soul, but only when you let go of your own efforts and rely on my loving care." The insomniac, forlorn and impotent, can become a gracious receiver of gifts.

Next time you are insomniac work with it as blessing more than curse. For example, you might use that time for the focused meditation and prayer that are so hard during a busy day.

Pajamas
Friend of Body and Soul

*E*ver stopped to think about pajamas? Probably not, or not too deeply. But you may spend twenty years or more of your life in your jammies (or other nighttime equivalents)—they're worth a few minutes of reflection.

Day clothes we often choose for their look more than feel. Men choke their necks with ties, and women their waists with pantyhose, all to what end? The impression we make on others. Only this could justify impressing such garments on our body.

Clothes, like people, have an inner face felt from within, as well as an outer face they turn to the world, and our emphasis is often on the latter.

Pajamas speak more to the inner face. We don't don them to impress colleagues at work—nor, unlike some other nightwear, to impress lovers in bed. Pajamas are more like being with an old friend. Like old friends they should be trustworthy, keep us warm on a frigid night. They should fit loosely so there's plenty of room to squirm around, shift position, be who we are without constraint. After all, we share with them some of our most vulnerable moments—curling up fetal-like to slip off into sleep, bedridden with illness, or stumbling to the bathroom. We neither judge our pajamas nor are judged by them, thank God.

Of course, you may don a T-shirt for bed, or nothing, a cotton nightie, or an old pair of sweats. It's all "pajamas" in the sense I use here. Clothing so comfortable it prepares us to let go, dissolve the ego-self into sleep's sweet oblivion. Our jammies are the friend we hold close on this journey.

We might do best to attend worship services in our pajamas. In fancy clothes we often feel constrained and on display, not the best way to meet our Maker. In pajamas we are more vulnerable, waiting like a child to be held.

Children were once taught to say this prayer: "Now I lay me down to sleep, I pray the Lord my soul to keep. If I should die before I wake, I pray the Lord my soul to take." Perhaps we should add another verse: "If God, my soul does call above, embrace me with your fervent love. I do trust so in Heaven's promise, that I'll be there in my pajamas."

When you put on your pajamas (or equivalent) tonight take a moment for prayerful gratitude to your old friend. Even better, make the donning of the pajamas itself the prayer, as you prepare for healing sleep.

The Belly Button

A Holy Place

*T*he belly button is a deep spiritual symbol. At first glance it hardly seems so. If anything the belly button is vaguely comic: a catch place for lint, an inviting spot to tickle, with funny little wrinkles forming "innies" and "outies." But look more closely. In fact, look through the belly button to what lies on the other side.

At one point (yes, literally at that one point) we were attached to our mother's body through the umbilical cord. When that cord was severed it left a hole, reminding us that we were once connected to a larger Whole. The navel is a holy place (a hole-y place?) residing right at the body's center. It speaks to both the loss that comes with individuality, and the call somehow to go home.

For we feel the hole not only in the body but in our soul. Somewhere, even in the best of lives, the most well-adjusted of personalities, is a sense that something is lacking. There exists a hole, an emptiness, a longing, an aching that yearns to be filled. We can't quite put our finger on this soul-hole, as we can on a belly button, but nonetheless it is there.

We often rush to fill that hole with worldly things. Excitation, ego, success. Food, drugs, alcohol. Sex, and the thrill of first love. Power, control, security. So many strategies to fill the soul-hole when often the best strategy is to leave it empty. It is a tunnel leading back to the Divine. When we plug it up with too much lint we block our passage through. Better to empty out in prayer and meditation; to rest in our unanswered ache; to grow still and listen to the silence. Let us feel the hole, and not fill it. *Never avoid a void.*

Spiritual disciplines are often thought of in terms of doing— good deeds, rituals, and the like. But the truest discipline is often to refrain from doing. In the emptiness we find our omphalos that connects us to Mother God.

What are the holy disciplines that make you hole-y—
empty enough for God to rush in? Are you placing these
at the center of your existence like the belly button in the
center of your body?

SHAPE-SHIFT
Pretend You Are in the Womb

BENEFITS: a feeling of deep relaxation, comfort, and connection

Lie down on a comfortable surface, probably a bed or long couch. Begin to imagine, as you relax your body, that you are a fetus floating in the womb. You are contained within something much greater than you, though it is impossible for you to fully understand it. Think of it as the Divine Mother—you are inside her body. Feel the soft surface you are lying on as the womb in which you are embedded. You are floating, floating, as if in a sea of amniotic fluid. You need do nothing. Your needs are all taken care of.

Imagine that you are breathing in through your navel. Here is where the breath enters. Imagine the breath as also containing within it all the nutrients, sources of energy, that are needed by your small body. (If you wish, imagine an actual umbilical cord that connects you at the navel to the Mother.) As you breathe in, receive all this through your belly. As you breathe out, imagine the oxygen and nutrients spreading through the rest of your body, down to your lower limbs, up to your upper body and head, infusing you with life and energy. You are loved, connected, and sustained right through the core of your being.

Note: If you wish, silently repeat the syllable OM or AUM (the Hindu mantra said to contain within it the whole universe) in time to your breathing. Hear the "O" as you breathe in (through your circular navel), and the "M" sound as accompanying the out-breath that spreads throughout your body. Imagine this Om as standing for *om*phalos or *um*bilicus, your connection to the whole.

Death and Birth

The Unlikely Twins

*T*he closest thing to death may be birth. How so? They seem to be polar opposites in the human life span. Let's look closer and from a fetal point of view.

Pre-birth, you are encased in a safe and familiar world. All of your needs are immediately filled. There's no incentive to seek radical change. But suddenly—oh, calamitous event—against your will you are projected on a journey. What will be the outcome? Into what universe, if any, will you come crashing? All the fetus knows is that its own world has come to a devastating end.

Yet seen by someone on the other side how differently things appear. Birth is a launch into freedom. From a constricted world, barely larger than itself, the newborn is catapulted into a much vaster space. So much to see! To taste! To do! How limitless are the opportunities once freed from the umbilical tether. This "catastrophe" has proven to be a liberation that was hitherto unimaginable.

It would make sense if life ended much as it began. Listening to a sonata, no matter how many changes of melody and key it explores, we wish to return at the end to where we started. So, too, with life—we crave excitement, novelty, unpredictable events—yet finally we want to come home.

And what if the end is like the beginning, death a recapitulation of birth? When death comes to take us away, we cry and mewl like the late-stage fetus, struggling to remain as we are. But the death contractions, like those of birth, cannot be denied. We are expelled from the womb of life, so secure yet so confining—but expelled into what?

Those who've come back from near-death experiences tell of a much vaster world. They speak of traveling through a dark tunnel (like the birth canal) only to emerge into a dazzling light where they are welcomed by beings of love. People who have experienced near death often report being loath to return to this earthly plane of pain and limitation—as loath as an active child might feel to be crammed back into the womb.

Our fearful imaginings make of death a contraction. To be buried underground in a sealed coffin seems a horrible confinement indeed. But what if death proves quite the opposite? What if it is an expansion, an explosion beyond earthly limits? We could no more understand such an after-life than could a fetus the universe it was about to enter. The two worlds are sealed off from each other, transitions between them unsettling in the extreme. Nonetheless, facing death, it may help to know that we've been through something like this before. Happy birthday!

Does this image of death make sense to you? See if it brings meaning or consolation. If not, ask yourself what other image of death might work better. Ask for inspiration, intuitive guidance.

Coming to Our Senses

Use your eyes as if tomorrow you would be stricken blind. And the same method can be applied to other senses. Hear the music of voices, the song of the birds, the mighty strains of an orchestra, as if you would be stricken deaf tomorrow. Touch each object you want to touch as if tomorrow your tactile sense would fail. Smell the perfume of flowers, taste with relish each morsel, as if tomorrow you could never smell and taste again. Make the most of every sense.

HELEN KELLER,
INTERVIEW IN THE *Atlantic Monthly*

I think it pisses God off if you walk by the color purple in a field somewhere and don't notice it.

ALICE WALKER,
THE COLOR PURPLE

Color

The Unnecessary Beauty of the World

*T*o learn about color ask a child. Or better yet, watch a child in action. The ecstasy of finger painting, the body itself become a brush; the subtle pleasure of sharpened colored pencils; the broad swaths created by a profligate marker; all in sky-blue, sea-green, and sun-bright yellow, the humor of orange, outrageous purple, earthy brown, fire-engine red . . . and on and on, dancing in celebration. It's as if the child—and only the child—grasps how wild it is that our world is in color.

After all, it didn't have to be. A black and white world would be perfectly functional, like the TV sets of old. This is what is perceived by certain color-blind species, and they didn't become extinct. Nor does their life-experience seem particularly deficient. Face it: Color just doesn't have to be. For that matter, neither does music, or roller-blading, or weaving flowers into a garland. The world is filled with extraneous beauty and unnecessary pleasures. We could get along without them, and often do. But God's creation is not just about functionality, like an office space designed to maximize worker productivity. Thank God (literally) that it's as much like an art gallery, a playground, a funhouse, filled with unwarranted joy.

As children, we dive into this exuberance. We truly see the world's colors and love them passionately, and love our ability to play with them as we choose. A box of sixty-four fresh crayons, each unique, with names like "burnt sienna" and "aquamarine"? Hey, it doesn't get any better than that. Unfortunately, all too often we lose interest as adults. "Put away your crayons," we remind the child, preferring a tidy room. Why look out the window? We've seen the blue of a sky, the green of an oak tree, so many times that frankly it's a bit boring. Instead we study stock quotes. We tap e-mails to one another, track world events. "What's black and white and red (read) all over?" goes a child's riddle. The answer: a newspaper. The sad thing is that while it's read, it isn't red, but all too monotone.

So let us live in living color. To soak in the bright hues of sky and grass; to appreciate the "local color" of the place we inhabit; to now and then go out and paint the town red: unnecessary but so life-enhancing. Nothing is more empty than a coloring book left blank. So be like a child—for that matter, be like God—and color in your world.

Pretend for a moment that the world is a coloring book that could have been colored in otherwise or left blank. For example, imagine how trees would look if they were red, and the sun if it were blue, or if both were just left white. Now look again, and see the world just as it is, appreciating its beautiful colors.

❖

God is beautiful, and He loves beauty.

MUHAMMAD,
PROPHET OF ISLAM

❖

Smell

The Mystical Sense

Smell is the least proud of the senses. It seems the dunce of the class, the one most likely to be mocked. After all, glorious sight surveys the distances, traversing thousands of light years as it views the distant stars. Hearing receives the celestial music of a Mozart, or a bird's golden trill. With touch we caress our lover's neck. Taste enjoys a subtle panoply of flavors. But smell? To open its flow we blow our nose. "You smell" is a schoolyard taunt.

Yet there is something indescribably precious about smell—even ethereal (from the Latin *aether*, for "pure air"). A smell wafts through the air, surrounds us, seduces us, slipping in through the window of the nostrils. Smelling is a bit like eating, but released from all that chomping and saliva. Instead, the scent insinuates itself invisibly into our body. Like an olfactory Tinkerbell, it diffuses about, wafting our awareness through time and space, as when the smell of suntan lotion calls up a long-ago beach day. Smell beckons like a finger then dissolves back into mist.

Unfortunately, we have grown so dense, and our environs so sanitized, that our sense of smell has diminished. The finger beckons and we barely notice, absorbed in life's sights and sounds. Watching a dog is the best recovery program. See it led by smell's lure to sniff at this scrap of garbage, that pile of poop, on its delightful olfactory ramble.

However diminished, smell still has the power to infiltrate the human heart. To lure a man, a young lady dabs on perfume. The scent is more subtle than reason. It rides the air, mingling with pheromones, and exerts an invisible pull.

So next time you are tempted to mock or dismiss smell, let us think of it instead as something mystical—a *misty call*. Since time immemorial we have imagined what God might look like. (Radiant light? An old man with a beard?) Or what God might sound like. (A voice in the whirlwind? Crash of thunder? A still, small voice within?) But rarely have we asked the equally cogent question—What would God smell like? We may not know the answer. (Incense? A pine grove? The scent of hard-earned sweat?) But we'll never find the answer, we'll never even find the question, until we remember to smell.

As you go through the day, remember to be alive to the smells that surround you. Just as you might work with your breathing as a meditative focus, returning you to the here and now, today work with your smelling.

If on earth there be a paradise of Bliss,
It is this,
It is this,
It is this.

FIRDAUSI,
TENTH CENTURY PERSIAN POET

Whispering

The Harmony of Speech and Silence

Nature loves to whisper. A breeze rustles the leaves. The thrum of cicadas rises and falls in vibratory cadence. A stream burbles over a rock bed. There are days when all creation seems to whisper, as if fearful of breaking a spell with sudden noise.

This, too, may be why we whisper to one another. We want to avoid waking a baby. Or we wish to preserve a tender message for the beloved's ear alone. Something precious would be smashed—like a crystal glass lying shattered on the floor—if the whisper became a shout.

For a whisper is the harmonizing of speech and silence. It is expressive—pressing out a message. Yet it does not disrupt the quiet like more forceful speech. Only the lips, the tongue, the breath come into play, not the reverberant vocal cords. As such, a whisper is speech/not speech. Or we might call it sigh-lence, silence that merges with a sigh, and with signs, eloquent in their expressiveness yet gentle as the wind.

When children whisper it makes the game they play more special, as if what was being communicated was too magical to be profaned with noise. So, too, a whispered prayer at the altar. Who would you trust more: a yelling, fist-shaking preacher, or one who whispers to an intimate God?

We might imagine God, himself, spoke forth creation—"Let there be light" (Genesis 1)—with a thunderous roar. That would surely get results! But shouldn't the first words that emerge from silence not destroy the silence, but somehow honor and preserve it? No, it's not likely God screamed at the top of his lungs. I prefer to think he whispered. Listen closely to the breeze in the trees; or the murmuring stream; or the sigh of your breath—and you'll hear that whisper still.

Try whispering like a child and enjoy the magical mood it creates. Also listen, as you go through the day, to any whispers that surround you, especially those of the natural world.

Bells
Hearing the Origins

*C*hurch bells, dinner bells, bells for meditation. Wedding bells, funeral bells, bells upon the hour. Why do we turn to bells to signal or celebrate exceptional moments? What is it in the sound of a bell that so rings the human heart?

Not only its rich, clear sound. We find that in an oboe. Not only the bell's reach across great distances, connecting a community through rhythm. We find that in a drum.

There is something else about a bell—something metaphysical. For a bell unites what is disparate in time. It is initiated in the sudden moment. Silence shatters when a bell is struck. A bell's advent is always shocking, grabbing our notice like someone unexpectedly seizing us by the elbow.

Yet its fade back into silence is gradual, like a hand caressing our sleeve ever more gently. Who knows when the hand is definitively gone, or the exact moment a bell stops ringing? As its pulsings fade away it seems like they may be going on forever –just more subtly than our ears can hear. In a sense, this is true. The sound waves keep expanding outward through space like ripples from a thrown stone.

In fact, physicists say, this kind of motion is the source of our universe. How did stars and nebulae, vast galaxies, and even vaster galaxy superclusters condense out of what was originally an almost perfectly homogenous quark-soup? One current answer: The Big Bang gave off waves, which, like the sound waves of a bell, initiated vibrational peaks and troughs. The peak regions of infinitesimally higher gravity began to attract a bit more matter to them, which in turn raised their gravitational density, attracting yet more stuff in a slow buildup of matter-rich regions. The rich got richer, the poor got poorer, as the universe distributed its goods over the last 13.7 billion years.

And that's not all. As Dennis Overbye writes in *The New York Times*, "The fireball [of the early universe] was, in effect, ringing like a bell, with a main note and overtones. The 'notes' on which the early fireball was singing give a direct way to calculate cosmological parameters like the geometry of space-time, the density of the universe and its rate of expansion" (May 24, 2002).

When we look at the nighttime sky, and even more so, map the large-scale structure of the universe, we see the vibrational aftermath of the Big Bang. Or perhaps we should call it the *Big Ring:* Our universe was rung into being.

Maybe we somehow sense all this when a bell sounds. The suddenness of the moment of creation—the infinite slow expansion of a world—the pulsing waves that create structure out of chaos, turning time and space into music: It's all there in each bell-ring.

So at christenings, weddings, funerals, by all means ring the bell. "Send not for whom the bell tolls," wrote John Donne. "It tolls for thee." In truth it tolls for all of us, this sound of the cosmos singing.

When you have a chance, listen to the sound of a bell ringing, or make one happen (a metal spoon and pot work well). Hear the sound of the cosmos expanding.

Sex

The Ecstasy of Creation

Sex. Many spiritual seekers are distrustful of it. We can forget spiritual pursuits, even moral constraints, in our search for lustful pleasures. True. But sacred traditions teach another lesson: Sex, properly understood, is an expression of the Divine, central to the miracle of creation.

In sex we make two into one. Of course, those engaging in sex do not lose their separate identities. Their distinctiveness, and the consequent desire for one another, is the source of sexuality's

pleasures. But central to sex is a penetration, a merging. This may be genital in nature, or just two hands holding, two lips kissing, a stroke of skin upon skin. Togetherness is experienced not just through a meeting of minds but an intertwining of eager bodies.

We are all born from such a merger (neglecting, for the moment, artificial conception). Two join to form one, and from this union comes a third. Cosmologists describe how our universe began with a Big Bang, exploding the one into separate beings. The Big Bang of coitus reverses this, reuniting the separate back to one. Yet, this in turn gives rise to new creation, as the one and the many do their dance.

"In the beginning was the word." Imagine that word as a cosmic "Yes!" not unlike the "Yes!" of the lover at the moment of orgasmic release. (No wonder God on the seventh day rested.) Human life is created through orgasm, when the self explodes beyond its limits. We can imagine the Big Bang as a divine version: God-seed bursts forth in ecstasy. Our world is conceived.

Some may find this train of thought offensive, even downright sacrilegious. But this is because we have severed the sacred from the physical. *We* severed it, God certainly didn't. Just look around at the natural world, where the birds and the bees do it—no other way to make new birds and bees. Creation and procreation are ever intertwined, so let us say "Yes!" to sacred sex.

Have you had experiences where sex seemed to have a sacred dimension? What was that like? Try to rejoin what our culture has rendered asunder, and see your sexuality as a powerful image and tool of Divine creation.

The Caress
Held Close by the World

From the time a baby is born—even, in a sense, before that—it is dependent on the mother's caress. It longs to be held as much as it longs for food. (The two are intertwined when breastfeeding.) In a famous psychology experiment, baby monkeys were separated from their mothers and split into two groups, one given cloth-covered dummy-moms to cling to, the other only wire-dummies. The latter group became particularly sickly and withdrawn, even died in large numbers. The cloth-moms afforded some comfort, but not so the wire-moms—they could not provide the sense of caress the little monkeys desperately needed.

Human beings are little different in this regard. We inhabit a hard-wired world and thus suffer. In early and later life we are often under-caressed and in frantic search for more. This quest, not fully understood, may take us to self-destructive places. A drug addict can get hooked on the feeling of well-being the narcotic or stimulant induces—a kind of total-body caress. Someone who visits a prostitute may be seeking not just sexual release, but the feeling of being touched and held that nowhere else is available.

Caress-deprivation may, in fact, be the source of much of our culture's sexual drivenness. At first, that seems unlikely. If anything, sexuality, at least media-style, is obsessively voyeuristic, focused on looking rather than touching. But Huston Smith (*The World's Religions*) wisely comments, "People can never get enough of what they do not really want." We never feel filled up by the endless images of beautiful men and women paraded before us. We always wish for more and to see more revealed. Maybe that's because looking at images is not really what we want. We want to be held and caressed.

What to do? A human partner is not always available to fill that need. Yet we can find caresses elsewhere, for example from Mother Nature. This mom knows well how to hold her children. Feel a breeze caress your cheek with a light and loving touch. Notice the trees swaying overhead, as if their leaves were soft fingers stroking you from a distance.

Or find your soothing in the human-made world. Ease yourself into a warm bubble bath: full-body caress by immersion. Put on a favorite piece of music: Its peaceful harmonies are an aural embrace. Slip into a satiny dress or a well-worn pair of blue jeans. Each holds you tenderly in its own fashion. Pull a blanket up around you as you settle in for sleep—any question why it is called a "comforter"? It throws its arms around you through the long, cold night.

Sometimes, when we're in a special mood, the whole world can feel like one large caress: the air in which we swim as a fish in water; the gentle trilling of birds; the food which pleasures the palate, then fills us up from within; the soft earth which supports our tread.

There is hope then for those of us who feel (and who doesn't?) that we're not held and touched quite enough. This very moment we rest in the Divine Mother's arms. We can learn to sense her caress.

Consider becoming a bit more pro-active in seeking caresses. Touch yourself in a loving fashion. Ask a loved one for a hug. Wrap yourself in a blanket. Feel the stroke of the wind in your hair and the sun on your cheeks. Soon you may feel more cared for.

Mind Well

Hard it is to train the mind, which goes
where it likes and does what it wants. But a
trained mind brings health and happiness. The
wise can direct their thoughts, subtle and elusive,
where they choose.

BUDDHA,
THE DHAMMAPADA

Each time we do something that raises consciousness, we lift sparks of holiness to new levels. . . . we cannot raise sparks in ourselves without raising those in the world, and vice versa.

DAVID COOPER,
GOD IS A VERB:
KABBALAH AND THE PRACTICE OF MYSTICAL JUDAISM

Pens and Pencils

A Word to the Wise?

*R*ight now I am writing these words with a pen. Miraculous instrument! Clutched between my fingers, it is but six inches long, maybe a quarter-inch in diameter. The words printed on its side announce nothing more than "round stic fine." And a fine thing it is indeed. Like a sorcerer's wand it is capable of weaving magic spells ad infinitum. These words I am jotting down. A to-do list. A Shakespearean sonnet. I can fill up notebooks with ideas, reminders, inspirations, all from the quiet mouth of this unassuming friend.

It waits patiently to do my bidding. If I put it away for a time I will hear no complaints. It may sit for months on end forgotten in some desk drawer. Still, the moment I grab it, it leaps back to life, ready again to make magic.

But since I am the master magician much depends on how I wave the wand. "In the beginning was the word." Each time I write or speak I participate as a co-creator with God, bringing ideas into material form. For words have import—they change things. Look at sacred scripture; Marx's *Communist Manifesto;* a love letter; an insult spoken in the heat of quarrel that can never fully be retracted. Words make the meaning of our world.

The silent pen or pencil reminds us to pause before this power. We should pray to use it wisely. Will our next word be harsh or kind? Will it illuminate matters, or obscure them in greater darkness? One thing is sure: Each time we pick up a pen, peck at a computer keyboard, open our mouth to speak, we seize a sorcerer's wand and begin to weave magic.

Now what did you want to say?

What words will you use today? Keep watch. Reflect on whether your words express well your higher self, God's co-creator.

Books

Mind-Melds and Virtual Realities

A book is a strange thing. For the duration of time you read, someone else's thoughts are inhabiting your mind. The words, the sentences tell a story, paint a picture, suggest a train of thought that is yours and yet not yours. We are fascinated by the more esoteric forms of thought-transfer involving ESP. But isn't the thought-transfer brought about by reading every bit as much a miracle? The ideas of a single person can enter into and profoundly influence the thought-streams of millions, and thus their behavior, and thus the world in which they dwell.

As a reader, it is marvelous that we can choose with whom to mind-merge. We can tap into the fevered imagination of the author of today's top thrillers. We may never meet him at a party but he's there to curl up with in the privacy of our bedroom.

Nor, in choosing an author to converse with, need we stop at the borders of the living. We can meld our mind with that of Jesus or Buddha; with Socrates roaming the Athenian marketplace; with Epictetus, the crippled Roman slave wrestling with how to make the best of a harsh world. We can travel to any land we wish, any historical period, and converse with the geniuses of that age— be entertained by their wit, enlightened by their insights, dislodged from our customary views by their brilliance and eccentricity. What a privilege and a mystery! Walk into any library or bookstore and you are surrounded by thousands of virtual realities waiting to spring to life.

Be careful which you choose. The book you select (or magazine, or daily paper) is about to subtly change who you are forever. "How many a man has dated a new era in his life from the reading of a book," wrote Thoreau. A 1960s slogan is "you are what you eat," but isn't it truer that *you are what you read?* So many of us spend so much time filling our minds with daily mayhem.

Open up the morning paper and along with your breakfast you swallow tales of murder, duplicity, and catastrophe. It's enough to give the soul indigestion. But then there are words that recall us to our better selves and lead us toward revelation.

What do you think of what I've just written? After all, these words no longer belong to me. They are ours, the product of a mind-meld.

Today, what mind-melds will you engage in through your choice of reading material? Is it bringing you pleasure, growth, and fulfillment? If not, you might play with some different selections.

Novels and Plays
Appreciating the Drama of Our Life

*E*njoying a work of great fiction, you find yourself thankful for its characters. You become passionately involved with the hero and heroine, live and die with their turns of fate. They are as real to you as your neighbor—realer in a sense, since the author has probably taken you deeper into their thoughts, hopes, and terrors than you've gone with the person next door. Even the book's villains are essential to the plot. You wouldn't wish them away. The bad guys tests the mettle of the good guys, pushing them to greater maturity. The sillier characters provide comic relief. And so it goes: In a well-crafted play or novel every element serves its role.

We might apply this notion to our everyday life. Consider God-the-Creator as author of the world. Quite a book. It includes some genuine heroes, people we know personally or as public figures. We are grateful for their presence in our lives. If religiously inclined, we may be thankful to God for creating and inspiring their virtues. The skill of the author shines through in such characters.

What of the scoundrels and small-minded people we encounter? They seem less reflective of divine authorship and may be messing up the story of our life. But isn't that tyrannical boss, or betraying lover, a *darn good villain?* Aren't they testing and challenging the hero (us) in interesting ways, advancing the plot, revealing and developing our character? In one sense, they may be "screwing things up. " Yet they too are essential to the unfolding tale. Dorothy needs three fault-filled friends, a deceptive wizard, and wicked witches to trigger her journey home. So do we all. A little reflection will show how much even our "villains" have served our progress of soul.

Hindus say this world is *maya*—a kind of magic-show, a work of fiction not fully real. In Shakespeare's words, "All the world's a stage, and all the men and women merely players." At first glance, this perspective seems to diminish life. Quite the contrary, a yogi would reply. If we take everything too literally (and not literarily) we are apt to be shattered by setbacks. They all feel so heavy and real. To see life as a novel allows us to appreciate its novelty. And if it's all a play we are freed up to be playful.

Ultimately, all the characters in a Shakespeare play— Macbeth, Hamlet, Falstaff, or Lear—are an expression of Shakespeare's mind. The many are dreamed up by the one. So, too, the world, ourselves and others, are penned from the mind of God. Admittedly, we cannot fully grasp our Author. How could Macbeth grasp his Shakespeare? At one point this character describes life as "a tale told by an idiot, full of sound and fury, signifying nothing." We know just how he feels. But to rise in perspective, to see life as a whole, is to know that it is more than an idiot's tale, and nothing less than a work of genius.

What villains and rascals have you known, what setbacks encountered? Can you see how they have propelled forward the story of your life and helped to develop your character?

The Computer
Model for a Well-Functioning Mind

❖

*The disunited mind is far from wise.
How can it meditate? How be at
peace? When you know no peace, how
can you know joy?*

BHAGAVAD GITA

❖

The computer can tell us much about effective thought. Admittedly, the machine itself doesn't think. It is a tool, a handmaiden, to the human mind and body, something we ourselves constructed. Nonetheless, our tool can become our teacher.

Take the *delete* function. We often marvel at the "memory" packed inside a computer but just as valuable is its ability to *forget*. Press delete and you can make a highlighted paragraph disappear—or the entire text, or the file or folder of which it is a part.

Why not install a delete button in your mind? Or else assume it's already there— you just need to use it more frequently. Perhaps you spend your morning trying to resolve a mistaken bill. You get stuck on hold for an hour, then waste forty-five minutes speaking with an incompetent employee representing an impenetrable bureaucracy. O.K., the problem finally gets fixed—but now what? You can fume and brood the rest of the day about time wasted, and share blow-by-blow your tale of woe with an outraged spouse or friend. But mightn't it be better just to press delete? It happened, it's over, it's gone. The more we clog up the screen of attention by rehearsing the grievance the more we waste valuable time.

A computer's word processing system is also good at **bold-facing** or *italicizing* text. You simply block off the passage, click the mouse or push a button, and suddenly the text is highlighted. Much depends on what we choose to highlight on our mental screen. Isn't it often the day's *frustrations*, precisely what we'd rather forget? We can choose instead to highlight *blessings, successes, and joys*. This changes radically the look of life's text.

Of course, making such mental changes is never easy. Our mind-computer may seem to have a *"default* setting" that actually stresses *faults*, our own and those of others. But computers also allow us to override such settings by entering intentional changes. We can remind ourselves to systematically focus on the good. Over time, this may even reset the default parameters of our daily thoughts and feelings.

So imagine that on your mental "toolbar," in addition to "File," "Edit" and other such categories, there's a category called "Mood." What is its default setting—"Low-level anxiety" or "Slight depression"? Imagine resetting it for the day ahead to "Joy" or "Calm" or whatever you prefer.

Still, there's a saying among computer nerds: "Garbage in, garbage out." Sometimes we hit the limits of what our isolated mind can do. We may find ourselves trapped within a limiting or self-defeating perspective. Luckily, today's computers can also leap beyond themselves by surfing the Internet. Through a telephone modem (or even more high speed modes of connection) we are linked to the minds of millions of others, part of a worldwide web. Suddenly we have access to far more information and guidance then we could ever create on our own. We've merged our mind with a greater consciousness.

Something like this happens when we pray, or meditate, or use whatever "modem" connects us to a Greater Mind. Call it God, the Tao, or your Higher Self, we are tapping into a source of inspiration beyond that of the ego. We can then "download" what we need for daily life.

You might ask what else your computer has to teach you? For example, do you need a mental "screensaver" for down-time relaxation? A surge-protector for moments you feel overwhelmed? A bookmarked "favorites" list, like that used on the Internet, of most-valued people, books, and activities? An "instant messaging" system that allows you to log on with God and receive immediate responses?

A computer, by itself, may be a mindless thing. But it can *remind* us how to live mindfully and well.

Imagine you are changing the default settings on your mental computer, or resolving to use certain functions more effectively. What mental changes would you choose?

The Worldwide Web

www.Connection

*C*onnection. We long for connection. A man sits alone in an empty room, then cannot resist picking up the phone and calling the office for his messages. It's not so much specific information he seeks. Any given message will likely prove trivial or just impose a new demand. Still, receiving messages bespeaks *connection*: someone needs him and reached out to communicate.

What, no messages? He turns on the computer, and checks e-mail. He scans the Internet for news of the day. Even if the news is disturbing he feels connected to the larger world, not so alone. Or he turns on the radio to hear a DJ rapping casually like a best friend sitting at the breakfast table.

When Rene Descartes, seventeenth-century French philosopher, decided to investigate what, if anything, is certain, he retreated into solitary chambers for inward meditations. He asked whether the existence of the external world could be doubted. Yes, he thought, for it might all be a dream or hallucination. But can I doubt the existence of my very self? Not really, he concluded. Even when doubting all, there must be someone doing the doubting, someone experiencing the stream of consciousness. So Descartes began with the undeniable reality of the self and only later inferred a world.

But Descartes may have gotten it backward in some ways. We need the world to confirm the self's existence. People see us, call us, speak to us. We are remembered, engaged, sought out, valued. Thus we come to feel we are fully real, that we exist and have significance.

Our self does not, first and foremost, develop in isolation but as part of a vast spider web of relations. Which came first, the spider or his web? True, without the spider (separate self) there is no web—yet the reverse is correct as well. Without the web the spider could not feed, and would soon thereafter cease to be.

On some level we sense how deeply we need the web. We thrill to the shivering filaments that keep us interconnected to a small circle of loved ones; a larger cohort of friends and acquaintances; the thousands or millions who dwell in our community; and even billions across the globe. The latest technology only expresses this drive to interweave our lives. It is an *Inter-net*, where we join a W*orld Wide Web*. We become selves linked up to countless other selves like a new cyborg species with one collective mind.

But what is the drive for connection that seems to power this all? Is it just an attempt to escape from existential loneliness? A way to fill an empty day with mindless chatter? Yes, yes, there's some truth to such accounts. But sacred traditions the world over say something further: that the urge to connect is primordial. Somehow we came from the One. Our memory of this union and our longing to return is a deep fact of our nature. We recollect our origins by re-collecting with others. Some seek this through experiences of communal worship, others through falling in love. Some seek sex, and lots of it, while others log onto the Internet. It's all forms of *yoga*—from the Sanskrit root meaning "to unite." It's an attempt at re-union, weaving our way back to the One by building that worldwide web.

Next time you log onto the Internet (if you're a user) pause to feel the mystical power of being able to commune with millions of minds. (Or else substitute another technology, such as telephone or TV, and marvel at the connections it permits.)

"Home"

What's In a Word?

"Home." The very word can carry us halfway there. It includes within itself "Om," the celestial sound that Hindus say contains all the vibrations of the universe. To chant or meditate upon Om is to reconnect with the Source.

Tibetan Buddhists, on the other hand, often meditate on mandalas (sacred forms) that symbolize the unity of self and cosmos. We find such a mandala in the "o" of "home." It is the one circular letter, that most perfect of shapes, each point on the circumference equidistant from the center. The "o" reminds us of the eternal source that lies at the center of creation.

Add the "h" at the beginning of "home" and you get "ho" or better, "HO!" a joyful noise. This is reputed to be Santa's song— "Ho, ho, ho!"—as he hands out gifts to the kiddies. Or a solitary wayfarer meeting another on the road might call out "Ho!" To thus find a companion is to be partway home.

After the "ho" comes an "m"—a sound made famous in our time by the soup jingle, "M'm! M'm! Good!" The "mmm" sound speaks to a kind of bodily contentment that comes bubbling up through the lips. The person who gives us our first womb-home, and then shelters us through breast and caress, is appropriately called "mom" or "mama." She is m'm, m'm good.

After the "m" of home, comes a silent vowel. Put them together to find the word "me" hidden away within "home." Finally, home is where I can be me. No pretense is needed to impress. I am loved and valued for being who I am.

The word "home" thus says it all. It speaks of the Universal Source from which I came, and in which I find joy, contentment, and acceptance. Watch a young child for whom laughter and play are as natural as breathing. She is at home. Or an aged person who has made peace with his life, and even his death. He is returning to the source.

Of course, we don't always feel at home but wander restless through this world. Working one job, we long for another. We wonder if there isn't a better boyfriend or girlfriend than the one we're still stuck with. In summer's heat we crave the cool of winter, and vice-versa. Whence the source of this perpetual discontent? Isn't it more than just a problem with this particular job, lover, or weather? We wrestle with a primordial sense of exile like an orphan displaced from her home.

But how could we feel so not-at-home unless we had known a home to begin with? The pain of exile speaks to something we have lost and fervently long to recover. We tell this story over and over in different forms. The prodigal son of the Bible wanders off. Pleasure turns to pain. Finally, humbled, he stumbles home. Dorothy clicks her ruby slippers together. She now knows "There's no place like home."

Dorothy's prayer is perhaps the prototype of all prayer, meditation, and chanting. I want to go home. Nothing else will do. I click the slippers—or finger the prayer beads, eat the wafer, count the breaths in meditation—and seek to find some way home.

Most who've taken the journey say there's a surprise. Home is not some faraway Oz, but where we came from, the Kansas deep inside. The word sums it all up: *Ho!* (listen joyfully)—*Om* (the sacred All)—is in *Me*.

So many words contain healing power. Pick one word to work with (for example, "home," or "peace," or "relax") and come back to it throughout the day, repeating it internally and seeking to embody it. (As a reminder you might make a little sign with the word, and place it where you are bound to see it.)

SHAPE-SHIFT
Pretend You Are Coming Home

BENEFITS: an experience of relaxation, calm, and comfort

Begin this meditation by finding a comfortable, well-supported position, and following your breath. You might choose a point to focus your attention on: either the air going in and out of your nostrils, your chest expanding and releasing, or your abdomen rising and falling with each breath. Begin to say to yourself the words "come home." On each in-breath say in your mind "come". All your vital energies that have been dispersed in the world are now being gathered up and coming back in. On the out-breath say the word "home." Enjoy the sonorous tones that include within it Om, the sacred Hindu word that symbolizes the universe and its Source. Feel yourself now fully at home, and send that out-breath throughout your body, especially to any areas of tension and tightness. Let the out-breath relax you as if you were coming home, kicking off your shoes, felling fully welcomed and relaxed.

To this rhythm of "come" and "home" you might wish to add a third word, "rest." Say this during the space that follows the end of one out-breath and precedes the next in-breath. This is a time for you to rest at home, rest in the healing presence of the Spirit. You will find that if you add this word, the space between breaths will naturally expand, and in turn that will deepen your breathing.

At times your mind will flit off hither and yon following flights of thought. When you realize you have gone a-wandering in this way simply use your mantra to re-collect. "Come home" reminds you to return to your spiritual center time and again, the place where you are welcome and safe.

Note: You might use the New Testament parable of the prodigal son as a backdrop to the meditation. This young man wandered away from home and squandered his father's inheritance while pursuing the pleasures of the senses and ego. When your mind wanders, imagine it is like that prodigal son going off again on its adventures. Once exhausted, the son wanted more than anything to come home and rejoin the father. This you do each time you return to your breath, and the Father's healing words, "Come home."

The Music of Mood and Emotion

It is something to be able to paint a
particular picture, or to carve a statue, and so
to make a few objects beautiful, but it is far
more glorious to carve and paint the
very atmosphere and medium through which
we look, which morally we can do.
To affect the quality of the day, that is the
highest art.

HENRY DAVID THOREAU,
WALDEN

Tears

Cleansing and Healing

*I*t feels good to cry. There's the paradox—crying is often an expression of sadness, even of devastation, yet somehow it can still feel good. We even speak of "having a good cry." Why? The answer is right there on the surface, yet deep, just as tears themselves flow from the body's surface yet express depths of emotion.

The short answer: Tears *cleanse*. They wash things away. This function is obvious when the eye reacts with tears to an irritant. You are walking down the street and the onrushing wind drives a speck of dirt into your eye. Immediately the tears begin to flow. They are a gentle mechanism to protect and soothe the eye's surface. Most importantly, they serve to wash away the speck. Without tears it would remain stuck there, doing more damage in the end.

Emotional tears are no different. Something has irritated the soul: a rejection, abandonment, or disappointment. Perhaps someone behaved with unexpected harshness, or a cherished dream lies crushed on the street. The heart breaks, the world caves in, if only a little.

Then thankfully, automatically, tears come. With them begins the process of cleansing and healing. By expressing (pressing-out) the inward grief, tears begin to wash it away. The pain starts to clear. Space is created for hope, just as a cascade of rain cleans out the air, freshening it for a new crop of sunshine.

Even tears of joy have a cleansing function, as we release a preceding anxiety. Will the operation be a success? Will I have a healthy baby? Will I be forgiven and understood by my friend? Tears of gratitude express our relief.

So there is a hidden commonality between tears of joy and grief. Even the former speak of past pain, and the latter of hope for the future. True despair (from the Latin, *desperare*, meaning "to be without hope") is met dry-eyed. No water, no flow, no change, no hope. Just an empty eye staring into the void, or forever shut. But tears cleanse our vision, rendering it again fluid and alive. They are the living waters of grace.

Nothing in the world
is as soft and weak as water.
Yet for dissolving the hard and inflexible,
there is nothing better.

TAO TE CHING, #78

When is the last time you cried? Today, in response to one of life's disappointments, allow yourself to cry, or if unable to (especially in the face of social training) simply imagine a crying child, perhaps yourself when much younger. Visualize yourself holding and comforting that child, but permit him or her to cry.

Cheerfulness

Learning to Cheer for Yourself

Yaaay! Cheering is a primordial act. From deep within an excitement builds, a joy, an enthusiasm, that finally erupts in a Mount Vesuvius of emotion. Hands clap, voice shouts, "*All right!!*" It bubbles up when our sports team miraculously comes from behind to win. When our child performs in a school play and actually remembers his lines. When a good friend, ordinarily a wimp, finally, finally, stands up for herself and hearing of it we say, "*Yes!*"

But why is it easier to cheer for another than it is for ourselves? Perhaps we think it immodest. Who, after all, but an egomaniac would celebrate his own accomplishments with cheering? We'd be embarrassed to be discovered in the act, as if masturbating in the public square.

Yet wait one minute—what if we're *supposed* to cheer for ourselves? Say to yourself, "Job well done!" (whether as parent, worker, friend, spiritual seeker) and you'll probably feel more cheerful. Why not? Literally, you're more full of cheer, having become your own cheerleader. This in turn makes you more able to cheer others without feeling threatened by their successes. You become more of an enthusiast (from the Greek *en-theos*, "a god within").

So cheer up. You can literally cheer yourself up by daring to cheer for yourself. (Don't wait for someone else to perform the service or you may wait a very long time.) Find something good you did, or you *are*, or three things, or five, and say, "Hooray! Hooray for me. That I am who I am. That I can be kind, generous, make silly jokes. That I accomplish what I do. That I have special talents and quirks. That I *try* even though I don't always succeed. That I hang in there. That I'm still growing and learning."

It's win some, lose some, in the game of life. But it's difficult to get too depressed when you have your own cheering section over on the sidelines turning cartwheels and shouting "Hooray!"

Do you permit a cheering section inside your mind? Are you willing to give it a try? Find five or ten things you've done in the last day, which, even if minor or imperfectly executed, are worth cheering for.

Love

The Limitless Ocean

*L*ove is a funny thing. On the emotional level it ebbs and flows. One day we feel a surge of love for our child that all but knocks our socks off. The next day we're about ready to strangle him. Like the surface of the sea, the feelings associated with love come and go in waves.

But the depths of love are something different. There, as in the ocean depths, the waters lie still and dark. Neither the breezes nor the light that dapples the surface can penetrate this far down. Our conscious mind may not divine the full extent of our love and our surface actions will not always express it, yet love rests there in the depths of the soul.

Because it is unmoved by surface waves, this is the love known as "unconditional." Here we don't stop loving our child, spouse, or friend, simply because that person did something annoying, or we're in a bitchy mood. Neither, the theologians say, does God stop loving us despite our faults. Perhaps our own capacity for love derives from this source. In our heart is a drop of that divine sea which brought forth and nurtures all life.

It may take someone moving away, or even dying, to help us plumb these depths. We're not then so plagued by momentary irritations. (Again, he left his dirty T-shirt on the floor!) The surface waves calm. We can now see more deeply into the vast reservoir of love that before was obscured.

Some might call this false memory or false sentiment. ("Now that he's gone you've forgotten what a pain he was!") Not necessarily. This love, for remembering what was best about the person, and about the relationship, may be truer than the trivia we obsessed about for years.

But what of those we live with currently and more closely? Must our love remain an untapped reservoir, inaccessible as the ocean depths? Yes and no.

Yes, in that there is nothing we need to do, or in a sense, *can do* with all the love we encompass. Simply know it is there. Know it is the truest and greatest part of the self, just as the ocean depths are greater than visible waves and shore.

Yet, in another sense, to understand the depths of love invites us to plumb them more fully. Your child refuses to go to bed. Frustration and rage build like cresting waves. Can you instead take a moment to become still, go inside? To lower a diving bell to that uncharted region of the heart where you love deeply in a way untouched by surface turmoil? Can you then speak or act from such a place? If so, you may find a way to defuse the disturbance, to calm the troubled seas.

In the New Testament Jesus is shown on a boat with his disciples as a storm threatens to capsize the crew. They panic and despair, but Jesus "said to the sea, 'Peace! Be still,' and the wind ceased, and there was a great calm" (Mark 4:39).

Love has this power to soothe a troubled world. Wind and waves can agitate the surface but from the depths of our heart comes calm.

In your interactions with one person today see if you can distinguish between the surface level (where there may be distance or irritation) and the depth of your feeling for them. Pause, take a breath, and try to come from that deeper place.

SHAPE-SHIFT
Pretend You Are the Ocean

BENEFITS: a depth of calm and concentration; contact with a greater whole

Feel your body as the ocean heading toward the shore. Don't visualize yourself *on* the shore, *watching* the ocean. You *are* the ocean. See the beach just in front of you. Feel your breath as the movement of your waters.

Each out-breath is a cascading wave. Feel the wave slowly crest within and crash onto the beach. With each in-breath, feel those streamlets on the beach gather up and be sucked back into your ocean-body until—building, building—they break again as a wave. Aaaah. Breathing in, re-collect the waters, breathing out, release the wave. Make this vivid by visualizing the ocean (is it day or night?) hearing the beach sounds, most of all, feeling the waves crest and plunge within.

You will probably experience your breath slowing and deepening, You may feel energized, for the ocean has great power. You may feel calmed; with each out-breath the collapsing wave releases tension. But as the ocean has many moods, so permit these in your body. Your breathing might grow still like the little waves that ripple at the shore's edge on a calm day. When more agitated, you may feel the breath-wave roar, thunder, and crash. It's all good. The ocean knows not right or wrong.

When thoughts come, imagine them as driftwood being tossed here and there. Or the mindless squawking of circling seagulls. Pay little mind. It's all a piece of the shore's sights and sounds, but soon overwhelmed by the ocean's power, and the hypnotic rhythm of the breath-wave.

In this meditation you identify with the ocean surface. But as the meditation progresses, you may also find yourself sinking down (perhaps through a point in your abdomen) down, down into the ocean's depths. Here, all is quiet. Occasionally, a sea-plant waves its tendrils, or a fish skims by, but mostly it is dark and silent. The waves (your breathing) continue to crash overhead, but now even that activity has grown distant. You are in a timeless place, a place of great stillness. Nothing disturbs the ocean depths.

Fear

The Hidden Messenger of Love

*I*f ever there was one, fear seems like an anti-God energy. "There are only two forces in the universe: love and fear. Choose." So goes a popular New Age tenet, and it has some validity. But this stark contrast conceals a hidden harmony. If fear is the opposite of love, it must also somehow be its mirror-image, that is to say, a *reflection* of love.

How so? Well, think about it. Or better yet, experience it. The next time you are in a state of fear, instead of resisting it (like some evil force that must be driven out), accept it. Even welcome it, embrace it. "Come forward fear, stay a while if you wish. You've doubtlessly brought a message. Let me hear it; I'm all ears." True, the messenger is anxious and breathless. His voice is cracking, palms sweaty, muscles twitching and tight. But listen not for the manner of delivery but for the content of the message and you'll find it concerns something you love.

Afraid a tragedy might befall your child—Why? Because you love him or her so much. Or less nobly, afraid of the roller-coaster dips in the stock market—Why? Because you love money, what you think it represents and can purchase. Security. Joy. Freedom. A better future. Nothing wrong with loving these. Afraid that the lump on your back may be malignant—Why? Because you love life. You don't want it ripped from your grasp prematurely.

So fear brings a message concerning something you love, coupled with a belief that this thing is under threat. The messenger all but shouts: *Run Away!* Or, *Fight Back!* Fear is a panicky friend, poking us with an elbow so we will spring into action.

Sometimes that's appropriate. Fear of an oncoming truck may save a life. But often the saying applies—"With a friend like this, who needs enemies?" The stress associated with fear can do far more harm than the things we are most scared about.

So how to *overcome* fear? Or better yet, how to get fear to *come over* to the side of Spirit? The answer is in how we receive it. Whereas fear urges us to *Run Away!*—instead stay still for a moment. Don't just do something, sit there. Hear the fear speak to you of what you love, that thing that seems so threatened. Then listen still more and you may catch a deeper message: You are worshiping idols. That is the ultimate source of your suffering. The thing you love is too finite, too contingent, too easily threatened by uncontrollable forces. You won't find true and abiding happiness through a stock portfolio; or a benign diagnosis of a scary lump; or a sports team narrowly escaping elimination; or even total investment in a person you love. All these are too limited, not built to last.

Spiritual teachers the world over agree on this point. Their manner of expression only differs slightly. "Give not your love to this transient world of suffering, but give all your love to Me" (Hinduism: Bhagavad Gita, Book 9:33). "All forms are transient: all forms are subject to suffering . . . one should understand . . . 'this is not my Self' " (Buddhism: from the Anguttara and Samyutta Nikaya). "Do not store up for yourselves treasures on earth, where moth and decay destroy, and thieves break in and steal, but store up treasures in heaven" (Christianity: Matthew 6:19–20).

Fear reminds us of this truth. It is ultimately a spiritual messenger cloaked beneath a dark hood. Listen closely, and it shouts "*Run Away!*—to God." Only when we dare to believe in—better yet, experience—a love so unlimited that it outruns all containers, can we fully outrun our fear. Until then we seek security in an insecure world. We pursue freedom while entangled in a web of confinements. We long for endless life, but know death awaits us. We race anxiously from love to love, ever in search of Love.

Next time you become aware of fear, ask yourself what is the thing you love that feels so threatened? Can you use this as a moment to run into the arms of God and this greater, abiding Love?

Joy
The Mothership Calling Us Home

❖

The strength of the forces of holiness and the destruction of the shells that imprison holy sparks depends upon joy.

RABBI NACHMAN OF BRESLOV,
NINETEENTH CENTURY HASIDIC TEACHER

❖

*I*n joy we experience the soul's exaltation. At such moments an energy too often suppressed is freed up and rises. Make no mistake about it, we do not simply manufacture joy: It is a part of our original nature. Just watch any child abandoned in play. She laughs at the world, thrills to a butterfly, or a grand game of peekaboo, or a well-placed tickle that must and must not end. Joy is a deep statement of who we really are. The question is, where does it go?

The answer is complex. Or perhaps the answer is that *we become complex*. Instead of enjoying butterflies, we collect them to impress our friends. We come to realize that a tickle is invasive of personal space, and we learn to respect boundaries, our own and others'. Peekaboo comes to seem a pointless charade. We know after all that the other didn't really go away. Why this silly game of pretend? All too often when growing up, we outgrow joy.

Abandoned joy swirls unnoticed around our shoe tops. During the course of our daily duties we stomp on our own joy, and that of others, countless times without realizing it. *Please hurry. This is important. Don't screw up.* We come to suffer from a syndrome endemic in modern society: Ecstasy Deficiency Disease (EDD).

But joy, patient and subtle, never quite abandons us. At an unexpected moment it will tug on our trouser leg. Late for work, we open the door to a stunning spring day: There it is, the touch of joy. A smooth coffee and conversation at the local cafe. Shooting a basketball and enjoying the swish. Going off to the movies and—surprise—being moved. Or climbing into a stinging hot shower after shoveling December snow. Quick, before we can stop it—there it is again—*joy*.

Just as quickly it may flee, but joy leaves behind its mark—the hint of a smile, a lightness in the step, a heart-swell of memory and hope. Memory and hope of what?

Maybe it's like one of those science fiction movies in which aliens land on earth and disguise themselves as humans. Over time the creatures assimilate so well they lose track of their original mission. They begin to act and think like earthlings. Their home planet fades from memory. Then one day a signal is transmitted that summons together all the creatures. The mothership has come to carry them home.

Our moments of joy are like signals from this mothership. Remember, they say, your true identity. Once you were a child. You were free and joyful. This is from whence you came, the planet Jubilation. You set off on a mission to conventional adulthood. It was necessary—you have learned much and grown—but your soul will never be fully content there. The gravity of this planet weighs you down. The joyful moment reminds you of that spiritual home to which you more properly belong.

So when you experience a joy, however fleeting, treat it as a message: The mothership is calling you home. Also, consider well your answer. To embark on that journey may involve changing settled attitudes, pursuing mischief, and in other ways courting unconventionality. It seems risky. You may feel a little alien. But dare you turn down the call of the mothership?

Ask yourself, do you intend to make time today for joy? Is it on your to-do list? Consider putting it there—engaging in at least one activity that makes you genuinely happy, and slowing down enough to make room for joy's unexpected tugs.

Sports and Child's Play

If God alone exists, how has this world come
to be? . . . Referring to this mystery [Sri
Ramakrishna] said: "It is His play, His Lila! A king
has four sons. They are all princes but when they
play, one becomes the minister, another the
policeman, and so on.
A prince, yet playing as a policeman!"

SRI RAMAKRISHNA,
NINETEENTH CENTURY HINDU MYSTIC

Angels can fly
because they can take themselves lightly.

G.K. CHESTERTON,
ORTHODOXY

Play

The Soul's Delight

Want to witness a profound spiritual exercise? Don't start with a solemn Eucharistic ceremony. Don't sit with Zen Buddhists on a rigorous meditation retreat. Don't marvel at a yogi's ascetic practices and rituals. No—begin by watching a kid on the playground.

Whooshing down a slide; wiggling along the monkey bars; running up and down a maze of ladders; hooting out at playmates; collapsing into giggles—so free, easy, joyful, present—here's a spiritual teacher for the ages (and the aged). Children seek out experiences of release and astonishment with an energy grown-ups have long since outgrown. Jesus said, "Be like a little child or you cannot enter the kingdom of heaven" (Matthew 18:3). To be in touch with the Light it helps to be light-hearted. Hindus say the whole universe was created as God's *lila* (dance, play). Its moment to moment re-creation is God's recreation.

How different this is from the typical Western view. The world can seem a heavy thing indeed when viewed as a battleground of good and evil, a testing ground for the soul. But the world a playground? Well, why not? Quarks cavort, particles zap in and out of being, galaxies fling out their arms. Maybe humans are meant to be both the audience for and participants in this de-light-ful game.

From this perspective, spiritual practices become less like disciplines and more like child's play. The priest intoning Christ's words over wine and wafer performs a kind of magic show. What is conjured up? Nothing less than God. The Zen monk focusing on the breath in and out, in and out, plays an exquisite game of awareness. The "winner" gets the prize of *satori* (enlightenment). Sacred traditions the world over play with chanting (like a child's sing-song), yogic body disciplines (like playing Twister), devotion to gurus (Follow the Leader), prayer to God (talking with an

Imaginary Friend), and obedience to God's will ("Simon Says . . . do this"). To see these as games is not to minimize their power. On the contrary, it may free up their power by removing our feelings of burden and resistance.

Too often we associate spirituality with heaviness, as if God particularly liked black garb, somber faces, and a funereal hush in his house of worship. Why? The soul, like a child, loves a good playground. Stand back and watch it go.

What forms of spiritual play seem to "work" for you? Might it help to see them less as work and to engage in them more playfully?

Feeding a Baby
Messy Growth

*I*magine (or recall) feeding a ten-month-old baby. You've got him strapped into the high-chair (a struggle to begin with) and are attempting to spoon rice cereal into his mouth. The baby craves the food. The only problem is *he wants to help*. As the spoon ventures near his mouth he keeps grabbing at it, as if to say, "Daddy, I can do it myself!" Yet he can't, really. When he gets hold of the spoon the result is a mess—food all over his face, clothes, and high-chair, not to mention his daddy. The spoon itself is then clamped in his mouth or thrown to the floor as an experiment. Daddy struggles to be patient with the baby still unfed.

This, religions tell us, is much what happens when we live in self-will. We interfere with the Cosmic Design by pursuing our agenda rather than God's. Even when our motives are good, we're still asserting "I can do it myself!" We grab hold of the spoon: "I want to get that job . . . run this project . . . tell that person what to do." The result? We end up making a mess on ourselves and those around us.

Still, maybe God accepts our willfulness, even likes it, more than we imagine. After all, what would Daddy have baby do: simply remain ever strapped in and passive? Certainly not. By trying to feed himself, though he may often fail, the baby gradually learns how to do so. Through play, experimentation, trial and error, he slowly develops new skills. The urge to seize the spoon is as powerful as that to eat and as necessary for his growth.

Similarly, we might say, God *wants* us to exercise our will. We are not meant to be spoonfed babies but active agents in making a better world. To do so we need a firm will. We need to learn to feed ourselves and those around us. The child thus becomes the adult.

To lapse into self-will is not a terrible thing. Okay, we grabbed the spoon prematurely. The food never made it to our mouth. We're still hungry. We made a mess. We screwed up. What else is new?

Time to clean up the spill as best we can and ask to be forgiven. We can pray for guidance and renew our intention to harmonize our will with God's. Face it: The parent simply knows better. But we weren't *bad* to grab the spoon. It's a part of growing up.

Where have you made a mess through the exercise of self-will? Try to view that time with a generous and forgiving eye, like a parent watching a baby struggle toward mastery.

Bubble Gum

Expanding the Spirit

*T*o a child, bubble gum is a mysterious, even a magical substance. It starts out pink and hard (at least the gum of my youth did). Then you chew and chew for a good long while. An initial release of sugar pleases the palate but sooner or later (usually sooner) that begins to wear off. Much of the allure of bubble gum is found after it has lost its taste but has gained in softness and pliancy. Then, with the right placement of the tongue, the right use of the breath, suddenly the gum expands in an ever-increasing orb, larger and larger—skin thinning—until it explodes past all limits. And you can blow another bubble, and another, and another. The gum itself has no limits but could in principle be worked forever.

It's actually a pretty good image of the spiritual journey. When you first experience God-contact (or whatever you choose to call it) things may be quite sweet. You taste joyful experiences of being guided and consoled by a Higher Power. Clarity comes where before confusion reigned. No longer alone, one feels loved and secure. This is like the sugar in the chewing gum that initially floods the palate.

But great spiritual authors attest that often this sweetness fades to be replaced by a time when the Divine is not to be tasted. Chew and chew upon the gum—pray, meditate, chant—use all the old techniques that once released the sweetness—still nothing comes. Just the texture of used-up rubber.

But that initial sweetness was never meant to last. True, it induced the child to first chew the gum, but if gum contained nothing but sugar and more sugar it would rot away the teeth. Similarly, if our spiritual life were nothing but sweetness and ease, our soul-teeth—that which enables us to probe, go deep, then absorb and digest—would rot away. We'd be left sucking compulsively on a sugar-teat.

Working a piece of gum makes it ready for a metamorphosis. One day, mysteriously, it begins to swell with the breath—take on the form of the sphere—expand like a universe—culminating in a Big Bang. Here's where it all gets *interesting*.

So, too, in our spiritual life. If we keep chewing and chewing (praying, sharing, reading, meditating, repeating the mantra over and again) one day we will find such bubbles growing. Bubbles of revelation. Bubbles of compassion. Bubbles of insight. Bubbles of joy. God-bubbles all, one after another, and at the most unexpected times.

The challenge is to not spit out the gum prematurely. Remember, you're seeking not just superficial sweetness, but the ever-expanding bubble. As any child knows, that's what's *really sweet*.

Was there a time in your life when the spiritual "gum" tasted sweeter? What exercises do you use to keep on chewing, even when the gum is not flavorful? And have you experienced any God-bubbles lately?

Buried Treasure
Searching for Spiritual Riches

What child is blind to the pleasure of a good search for treasure? Many a pirate tale involves buried treasure on a desert isle and the need for a map to find it. The archetypal power of this story may point toward buried meanings for which we ourselves need a map.

A first question to aid our search: What is the ultimate treasure sought by people the world over? Spiritual texts call it God, nirvana, enlightenment, salvation (choose your term). Once found, this is a fount of riches capable of fulfilling our every need. Jesus speaks of the pearl of great price. Now imagine a pirate's dream of such pearls, gold coins, and brilliant jewels heaped one upon one another, a metaphor of spiritual wealth.

But to locate this treasure is no easy thing. In the words of Shankara, an eighth-century Hindu mystic, "A buried treasure is not uncovered by merely uttering the words, 'come forth.' You must follow the right directions, dig, remove the stones and earth from above it, and then make it your own." How best to do this can be difficult to discern. Should I work harder to claw my way toward God? Should I instead relax, and learn how to *be* rather than *do*? Should I cultivate my compassionate heart, or develop detachment from the cares of the world? We need a treasure map to guide us on our journey.

This is supplied in abundance by the world's religions. Hinduism speaks of the four yogas, diverse ways to unite ourselves with God. Buddhism traces out an eightfold path guaranteed to lead to enlightenment if we pace it off with diligence. Christianity sometimes distills it all into two steps—love God and love your neighbor as yourself which will lead us right to the treasure.

But written somewhere on each map should be a cautionary note. No path can be prescribed in advance to be followed identically by all souls. If you love God, that self-same God will give you further directions upon contact. Look within to discover which of the yogas is right for you. Teachers will arrive when the student is ready, both inner and outer guides. It's like the hero of a pirate story who is sent to a tavern, knowing there he will meet a one-legged man who will tell him where next to go.

In a sense, the treasure is the same for all, realization of the Divine. But the adventure meant for you is different than for anyone else, and can only unfold step by step. You must tread the one path that no else can ever travel: *the path that is your life.*

In the development of your spiritual life, what twists and turns has your treasure map led you on? Now, in a meditative state ask for another portion of this map to be revealed—where do you go from here?

Football

Moving the Ball Downfield

In football there are two ways to advance the ball downfield. The first, and by far the more spectacular, is the forward pass. The quarterback flings the ball with velocity and precision to a receiver who, with blazing speed, has outdistanced the poor defender. The gains can be substantial. With one seven-second play a team can move from deep within its own territory to the other team's goal line and beyond.

The crowd loves it. Players love it. And we love when it happens in our own life. Buried in a boring job, we dream of the promotion that can suddenly give us our heart's desire. Frustrated with a series of unsatisfying relationships, we await our dreammate who will change everything forever. Then there's hitting the Lotto, getting the promotion, having that mystical, spiritual breakthrough. These are so many versions of the dramatic forward pass, and some of them might succeed. But too often throwing the bomb is a set-up for an incomplete pass. We're still second and ten, then third and ten, then punt, having failed to move the ball.

Most football fans would agree that a good passing game must be set up by establishing the run. The run is that other less glamorous, but steadier and more predictable way of moving the team downfield. The quarterback simply hands off the ball to a hunk who barrels forward. The gains are more likely to be four yards, rather than forty, but put four yards together three times in a row and you've gained a precious first down. That allows you to keep possession of the ball, and run another set of plays, and so forth, down the field, until the goal comes in sight. It is a slower process than the dramatic pass, and from time to time it's good to mix it up and fling that long bomb. But any game plan needs balance, and the key to controlling the flow is to block, tackle, and run.

So, too, in life. Yes, those long-range passes will happen from time to time and lend our life exhilaration. But so often the day-to-day rhythm involves simply running the ball. A few yards and a cloud of dust. Pick up the groceries, pick up toys in the living room, pick up the kids at school, pick up the mood of your tired mate, and don't forget to pour a little pick-me-up at day's end. So mundane. But what's important is that you are advancing the ball, slowly but surely, downfield. And so, too, when you pursue a degree at school. Or work to master the basics of your job and put in a good performance. Or say your daily prayers, do your meditation, even when no dramatic experiences result. What's important is to keep advancing the ball, four yards, by four yards, by boring four yards, downfield toward your life's precious goals.

Pause to give yourself credit for the ways you run the ball downfield in your life. So it's not spectacular and no one's applauding. You can.

Sudden-Death Playoffs

Playing With Death and Eternity

When a sports team is playing for its very life we call this a "sudden death" game. A single goal by the foe, a last-second basket—any form of loss, heartbreaking and final—brings the season to a crashing close. The team is history. It goes home for the summer (or winter, as the case may be). The team that emerges next year will never quite be the same as the previous. As in the Buddhist notion of reincarnation, there is overlap, clear causal connection, between the two entities, but they are not one and the same. You cannot step into the same river twice, Heraclitus said, for it is constantly changing, and so, too, a sports team, with its trades, retirements, vagaries of performance, and other alterations. When the season ends, it is irrevocably over. Death has struck down forever that team (say the Buffalo Sabres of 1993), and symbolically all of its members and supporters. They descend into Sheol, the pit described in the Psalms, where the dead lead a bleak and shadowy existence. Hence, the profound misery of the disappointed fan, and most fans do end a season disappointed.

But what of the winning team, which by valor, luck, or skill survives the battle and goes on to the next round? If the losers experience sudden death, the winners taste of perpetual life. They live to play another game and another, advancing deeper in the playoff rounds, and if only they can keep on winning they will emerge as champions. True, at that point the season ends even for them. (Sadness, that uninvited guest, lurks about the edges of the most exuberant champagne celebration.) But in another way, death is defeated. Forever that team will be celebrated. For example, the Los Angeles Lakers won the NBA basketball title in the 2001–2002 season. This cannot, will not, ever change, as it echoes down the corridors of time. It is recorded in the musty books of sports lore. It will live on in the memories of avid followers that retain, as if in perpetual slow motion, that masterful dunk by Shaquille O'Neal. The players are immortalized forever as champions, frozen in time, even as the real Shaquille and his teammates turn gray, bald, or plump around the waistline. The real men are not quite the real thing; the Platonic perfection of their feat, their de-feat of other teams, of fate itself, keeps them in video and memory forever triumphant and alive.

So what are we really battling for in sport? Why do pot-bellied fans scream themselves hoarse in arenas the world over and in front of TVs? Why so much passion, such intensity, as if nothing could possibly matter more than the outcome of this children's game played by hired hands who will probably switch teams next year? (The non-sports-addicted look on in bemusement.)

It's because what is at stake is nothing less than eternity. Will we die suddenly with the losers? Or will we live on, and on, joyfully and forever?

This is a central existential question for every human being. And so it is for sports fans, who in ways unknown even to themselves, are playing ball with the Eternal.

If you're a sports fan, try watching a game as if it were your yoga—your method of spiritual union. That is, try watching the game prayerfully, or as a form of meditation, and working with the intensity of the desires and emotions that arise. (You'd be surprised at the spiritual content that can emerge from watching the game, and watching your reactions to it.)

Balloons

Death as Liberation

*P*op a balloon and you will see a child's face sag. Like the balloon itself, all the air goes out of the child as she clutches a pitiful piece of rubber where moments before there was glory. How could something so joyful, so birdlike, be reduced to this pathetic scrap of rubber? Was the balloon but illusion, an illusion now popped? Or if the balloon was real, and surely it was, where oh where has it gone?

The truth is that the magic of the balloon lay not in the rubber but in the air. By itself the piece of rubber was next to nothing. Literally. It is the "nothing," the breath, the air, that stretched its boundaries, forming a sphere; breath pushed the balloon upward, beyond the earthly plane; breath made of it something lighthearted, uniting this world with the celestial. When the balloon pops it may be a misery to the onlooker, a collapse to the rubber, but to the breath, a liberation. It has exploded beyond the limits of the balloon-skin. No longer confined, this air mingles with the air of the universe, brother greeting brother.

And perhaps this is the best image we can have of dying. To the onlookers it is a tragic event. A human being so filled with the breath of life collapses like a popped balloon. The magic departs. We're left with a pitiful carcass already beginning to decay. Where did the spirit of the person go? Was their life, their joy, their love, but an illusion now thoroughly destroyed? We cluster around the deathbed with sagging faces like children around a popped balloon.

But let us remember that the true balloon is not the rubber but the breath. Upon dying, that breath of life (and words like "spirit," and "psyche" all come from the word for "breath") is not destroyed but liberated. With a loud pop, both sad (for what has ended) and joyful (for bursting past limitation) the spirit can expand beyond earthly confines and rejoin the greater realm.

We are sad when the balloon pops, but the balloon is not sad. It pops much like a champagne cork.

See if this image of death works for you—does it resonate with your beliefs and experiences? If so, think about the death of a loved one, or your own future death, in these terms and see how it shifts your feelings.

Pretend You Are a Balloon

BENEFITS: deep relaxation; a sense of unity with the One; diminished death anxiety

Sit in a comfortable position, perhaps on a chair or cross-legged. Alternatively, you may wish to lie down. Loosen any constrictions around your waist so you can breathe deeply.

Now imagine that your belly is a balloon. Pretend your navel is the opening to the balloon. With each in-breath pretend that somebody is blowing gently into that hole, expanding your balloon with air. (Physiologically, this will encourage use of your diaphragm, rather than your chest muscles, in breathing. To aid this switch to deep abdominal breathing, place your tongue on your upper palate and breathe through your nose.)

As your balloon is blown up with air feel your belly expand. Imagine it is made of elastic so there is little resistance to stretching. When your balloon has reached a comfortable size (don't force it) feel the air start to seep out your belly button as the balloon collapses. Release all tension from your body.

As you continue this style of breathing, you may experience your inner balloon becoming even more stretchy (as a real balloon might with repeated usage) so that you breathe more deeply. Let the balloon now encompass your belly and chest—even your torso, head, and limbs—all expanding and releasing with each breath.

Finally, allow your body-balloon to pop. Imagine this either as a forceful pop or a gentle one where the air seeps out of a small puncture. Let your body sit or lie still like a collapsed balloon. Focus your attention instead on the air of your breath now releasing from your body, from any container whatsoever, one with the space of the universe. You might imagine it as a wind sweeping over the ocean surface, whistling through a mountain pass, or floating above the clouds. Experience the newfound freedom as you breathe, no division between self and world. Enjoy being one with the All.

Note: To enhance deep relaxation you might imagine yourself as breathing into three balloons, filling one after another: first your belly balloon, the second in your chest (as your ribs expand), and then the third toward the very top of your lungs behind your clavicle. This brings about a deep three-part "yogic" breathing.

Home Run
The Journey Home

❖
---

*Since baseball time is measured only in
outs, all you have to do is succeed
utterly, keep hitting, keep the rally
alive, and you have defeated time.*

ROGER ANGELL,
THE SUMMER GAME

❖

What is it about the home run? For true aficionados of baseball it is not the most elegant of plays. That honor belongs more to the subtleties of the game: the perfectly laid down "suicide squeeze" bunt that brings a runner scampering in from third; the deftly turned double play executed in mid-air by a pivoting second baseman; the diving grab of a sinking line drive by an outfielder almost out of breath and time.

Yet the home run stands by itself. Among baseball moments it is towering, exclusive. It somehow surpasses all mortal events, no matter how wonderful, that take place on the field. For the home run is transcendence incarnate.

The batter begins by facing a nearly insurmountable task— hitting a small orb thrown at velocities up to one hundred miles an hour, its path angled by spins and dips. Sometimes life can feel like that. We try hard to hit the mark but life throws us round-house curves and darting fastballs, combining both speed and deception. Yet every now and then we *connect*. The home run is the epitome, an almost miraculous event. The ball, an earth-bound spheroid, is suddenly transformed into an airy bird soaring beyond all limits. Ground gives way to sky, flesh to spirit.

In our finest moments we know something of this feeling. Our heart soars. Our feet float above the ground. We wish such exhilarating moments could last forever.

Yet all too often we end up tumbling back to earth. A first love slides into boredom; a high gives way to a hangover. It is like the towering fly ball that settles in the fielder's glove. When all is said and done, just another out.

Ah, but not with the home run. There dream becomes reality. It embodies the Buddhist chant, *"Gate, Gate, Paragate, Parasamgate, Bodhi Svaha"*—Gone, gone, gone beyond, gone completely beyond, hail the awakened one! For the home run has gone beyond the players and their reaching gloves, beyond the fences, beyond the very field that defines the game. All hail the man or woman who has accomplished such a feat. Fifty thousand fans rise as one.

They rise, that is, if the homer was hit by the home team. For finally, the home run is not just about a magical journey to a distant land. It turns out—and here the paradox—that this journey is all about coming home. He or she who hits the homer is not stranded on base like so many of us, waiting, hoping, partway there. The home run hitter completes the journey—of Odysseus, of the prodigal son, of countless heroes who leave home and wander the four corners of the wide world until, transformed by the journey, humbled but triumphant, they finally come back home.

For the solo home run hitter this return is marked on the scoreboard by a glorious *One*. In coming home, we realize the One—the Transcendent that unites us all. But for such reason, a person who has come home—a Jesus, a Buddha—also has the power to bring many others with him. Everyone on base, all who engaged in the needed preparation, are brought to fruition by the savior. They come home together, dancing and clasping hands. And all the fans, the disciples, share in the high-five. Yes, all hail the enlightened one who has transcended all limits, lifted all burdens, shown us the possibility and the path.

We long for our spiritual home. The home run promises that it is there for us, though far from easy to attain. We must prepare, be patient, and work long hours in batting practice. But if so, one day we will step up to the plate—clear our vision—find our footing—take our full swing—connect!—and embark on the journey that carries us outward yet finally brings us home.

Image your spiritual life as a baseball game (if you can relate to this); what base would you be on now in your journey around the base path? How did you get there, and how do you see yourself coming home? (Through a series of singles? Good teamwork? Can you imagine the possibility of hitting a home run?)

Merry-Go-Rounds
Coming Home to the Divine

❖

God is a circle whose center is everywhere and whose circumference is nowhere.

ATTRIBUTED TO EMPEDOCLES,
ANCIENT GREEK PHILOSOPHER

❖

My daughters are fascinated by merry-go-rounds. I wonder why—is it the painted animals, the bright music, the spectacle of this vast machine? Yes. But I suspect it is also something more, something hinted at by the name "merry-go-round." Merrily, the animals *go*. Yet in their circular movement they always come *round* again to where they first began. They are going and coming, coming and going, and one suspects that if the overseer didn't call a halt, the circular dance might last forever.

Black Elk said, "Everything an Indian does is in a circle, and that is because the power of the world always works in circles, and everything tries to be round." There is a perfection about the circle. To travel in a circle is to accomplish what seems impossible—the union of movement and rest. The gears click in, the music begins, and with a joyful jolt, the merry-go-round starts turning. Yet it finally goes nowhere at all. It is anchored in the same place. Its horses remain, like all points of a circle, ever the same distance from the center. And though the horses seem to gallop off in one direction, they end up right back where they started.

The turning child waves to Mommy or Daddy standing near the merry-go-round. Is it a wave of hello or goodbye? Both. The child is both coming and going.

And such is our relation to God, the Father/Mother of us all. In our life's journey we ever seem to depart, leaving behind the Source. We become entangled in brightly colored webs of fascination: successes and failures, joys and miseries, jobs gained and lost, marriages and divorces. We ride the painted horse up and down. The Hindus call this *maya*—the magical, seductive melodrama of life that we take to be so real.

Yet for mystics what remains most real is our connection to the One. That karmic journey which carries us away also leads us to union with the divine. The prodigal son wandered far off from his father and became lost, hungry, and forlorn. Yet this suffering is precisely what turned him around and started his journey back home.

To believe that however far we travel we will once again glimpse the shining face of the Parent . . . regain our bearings . . . locate, in a turning world, one unchanging point of love . . . discover our leave-taking was but a disguised form of home-coming: This can sustain us on the journey. This can make life truly joyful, a genuinely *merry*-go-round.

What's most real, finally, is not that painted horse. We know it to be pretend. Nor the music—we know it is piped in. Nor all the up-down-roundabout tumult—we know it carries us nowhere. But the Shining Face that we ever glimpse anew—this alone is *real*.

Imagine life as a merry-go-round. Can you look past all the ups and downs, the painted horses and brass rings, and catch a glimpse of the Shining Face?

FOUR

The Universe, Our Home

Heavenly Physics

Now, my suspicion is that the universe is not
only queerer than we suppose, but queerer than
we *can* suppose.

JOHN HALDANE,
POSSIBLE WORLDS

When I was a child, I learned that the moon
was the goddess Dewih Ratih. Then Neil
Armstrong landed on it. I still look up at night
and pray to Dewih Ratih.

SURADNYA,
BALINESE ARTIST,
FROM *SIMPLY LIVING: THE SPIRIT OF THE INDIGENOUS PEOPLE*

Sun and Moon
The Loving Eyes of God

❖

Each one of us must make the discovery on her or his own . . . that God invented the universe to delight us. That his love is so much for each one alone that it seems as if the moon and stars had been made for our nursery windows and no other creature had occupied God's mind since time.

EMILE GRIFFIN,
CLINGING

❖

The sun and moon do a complicated dance that weave together night and day. It is evident that they are well-suited as dance partners. They appear the same size, a strange coincidence we tend to take for granted. The sun is a gas ball some 860,000 miles in diameter. By comparison, the moon is but a tiny 1,080 miles across, about 1/800 the size of the sun. But perceptually it makes up for its small form by its proximity. Whereas the sun flames forth some ninety-three million miles away from Earth, the moon is just a couple of hundred thousand miles away. For no discernible reason, comparative diameters and distances exactly cancel out, such that the size of the sun and moon appear the same from Earth. We see this illustrated most forcefully in a solar eclipse, where the body of one fits perfectly over the other in a once-in-a-blue-moon (black moon, really) wedding.

Yet, if married in form, sun and moon do so as complementary opposites. Sometimes the best marriages, or at least the most interesting, are between opposites. If the sun is gold, the moon is silver, echoing earth's precious metals. The sun brings warmth and light to the day. The moon illuminates in coolness the night. The sun is absolutely necessary to life. The moon seems gratuitous, an unexpected gift. The sun's glare is somehow aggressive, masculine. The moon's rhythms seem tied to the menstrual cycle of women. The sun is ever constant in shape, the eternal circle. The moon waxes and wanes, an image of ever-changing time.

To gaze upon these celestial partners is to see the two eyes of God watching over us with love. Without the sun there would be no day, no living earth, no creation as we know it. "Then God said, 'Let there be light'; and there was light"—that is, God said let there be *the sun*.

Yet the moon, less essential, more frivolous (like a playful wedding gift, not at all the practical sort) nonetheless comes bearing its own special favors. It tells us of change, of beauty, of illumination even in dark times. It is the patroness of lovers and poets. If the sun is the ultimate artisan, making all things, the moon is the aesthete, inspiring artists with its mysterious dance of veils.

Together these dance partners remind us that all is gift. That the blessings of earth are first bestowed from the heavens. That we are not alone, but go through life guided and graced by companions. That eternity and time mate together, male and female, day and night, sun and moon, sky and earth—and that we are the offspring of their marriage. We need only look up to see our Father or Mother, and feel ourselves as babes in the crib watched over by loving eyes.

Try seeing the sun and moon today as the eyes of God, watching, nurturing, and protecting you and all creatures on Earth.

Stars

Gazing Upon the Infinite

Starlight, star bright, first star I see tonight, I wish I may, I wish I might, have the wish I wish tonight. Why do we wish upon a star? Maybe, in some dim way, we know that the stars have granted all our wishes—in fact, they have wished our whole world into being.

In medieval times, this knowledge was expressed through astrology, the theory that stars in their course guide earthly events. Modern science tells us a different but related story. It is in the furnace of dying stars, and only there, that sufficient heat is generated to fuse together atoms such as carbon, oxygen, nitrogen—so crucial to the human body—as well as that of trees, birds, and all other organic beings. Life is truly a gift of the stars.

How wonderfully incongruous. The stars, so distant, so other-worldly in their shining, are the authors of our solid flesh. When we gaze up at the night sky we look into our own genealogy. We are star-beings gazing back at ourselves, mirrored across thousands of light-years.

By comparison, the sun and moon are mere neighbors. Only when they humbly shuffle off the stage does the curtain fully open on the splendors of the universe. Why do we not sit in stunned silence beneath the night sky, then explode into applause? Astronomers estimate that there are seventy sextillion stars in the visible universe. Think of it as seventy thousand million million million, or a seven with twenty-two zeroes after it. What mind, after all, can make sense of such vastness? What eye can take it in? And yet we can, and do, to some small degree. Near infinities of time, space, and number somehow register in the stargazer.

This also serves as a metaphor for the relation between self and God. As the small eye gazes upon a vast universe, so the small "I" can look to God. This is possible because the seer is somehow derived from the seen. The atoms of our eye were forged in exploding stars. So too our "I" is like an atom from the God-explosion that gave rise to the universe. In our finite self there remains a seed of the Infinite. This rests dormant through our ordinary days, like any seed waiting for its season. But at certain moments—in prayer, perhaps, or while listening to a Bach cantata, hiking in the wilderness, or looking up at the stars—that seed is watered, comes alive, and begins to grow and grow, until, like some miniature Big Bang, it explodes again, strewing our mind across the universe. We reclaim our kinship with the Divine.

From dust we have come, and unto dust we shall return—yes, but it is *stardust*.

Take a couple of minutes to contemplate that your body, your food, your house, your neighbors, are all made from stars. How does that change your sense of this world?

> *We bear the universe in our being as the universe bears us in its being. The two have a total presence to each other and to that deeper mystery out of which both the universe and ourselves have emerged.*
>
> THOMAS BERRY,
> THE DREAM OF THE EARTH

Celestial Space
Where Is God?

How can we misplace something as large as a galaxy? For example, the Andromeda Galaxy, though containing hundreds of billions of stars, appears as but a faint smudge in the night sky easily missed without a telescope. The reason is that, though our nearest major galactic neighbor, it's still some fourteen trillion miles away.

On the spiritual level, a similar issue arises. How can we misplace something as large as God? God is thought of as the source of all the universe. God's power and knowledge are similarly assumed to be infinite, dwarfing that present in the human sphere. And yet when we seek to contact this God, He/She/It can be awfully hard to find. Rarely does God roar from a whirlwind or set a bush ostentatiously on fire. What contact we achieve is often subtle, transmitted by a still, small voice within. To hear it we must grow still within, just as an astronomer must gaze quietly into the darkness, open to the sky's faint lights.

Perhaps much the same principle is at play. The stars cast little light upon us because they are so distant. In fact, without this distance we could not survive the nuclear explosions that fuel the stars or the gravitational fields that surround them. Similarly, could we survive a God who everywhere loomed over our world like a Gargantuan? We would risk being blown away or sucked into the vortex. How could we establish our individuality? How could we attend to the mundane details of our life? How could we exercise free will if God was ever intervening, like a child sticking his hands in an ant farm?

No, it is good that God withdraws in a sense, becomes still and small, the pursued rather than the pursuer. It gives us room to exercise our powers. The self, like our little planet, needs space to unfold. Thank heavens for celestial space.

You may have thanked God for specific ways He/She has been present in your life. Have you ever thanked God for being absent, and giving you space to be yourself, exercise your will, and grow into your full personhood?

The Night Sky
Death as Revelation

"*D*o not go gentle into that good night . . . Rage, rage against the dying of the light." So begins a poem by Dylan Thomas. But press on with this analogy between life and light, death and night, to challenge the poem's premise.

In the daytime our visible universe is lit up, but also limited by the sun. Its bright glare obscures the stars. Someone unfamiliar with night would assume that after sunset nothing is left—just blackness. So do we imagine death, and hence rail against it. Life, like the sun, dazzles us such that we cannot see beyond its margins. It's logical to think that when life departs consciousness ends. Nothing remains, just blackness.

But imagine the surprise of someone seeing for the very first time the night sky. The sun sets to reveal an unimaginably vast universe. The stars that number in the trillions are as if the material expression of an eternal essence without limit. The illusion that all would disappear with the sun is exposed as just that—illusion. On the contrary, the smallness of the visible day-world was itself the misleading deceit.

So, too, it may be with life and death. Life dazzles us with its rewards and demands. We are sucked into the play of time. But what happens when life, like the setting sun, departs? If the analogy holds, something amazing will shine forth. Call it the Unlimited, the Source, the Eternal—how can our minds grasp an immensity that transcends both space and time?

Of course, the day-world and night-world are finally one. The sun, which blocks other stars from view, is itself a star. Similarly, our own life is one creation of the eternal energy that lies beyond life and death. "Every being in the universe is an expression of the Tao" (Tao te Ching, #51).

Still it's easy to miss the bigger picture. Our time on earth can obscure the eternal, as the sun can obscure vast galaxies. We're blinded by the light. The gift of darkness is to enable us to see farther. The darkness of night—and of the grave.

Entertain the thought that death may open up a much vaster, spiritual world. What would be our attitude to our own death, and that of loved ones, if we really held to this thought?

Light

The Eternal in Time

*S*tudying physics the other day, a strange and wonderful fact came to my attention. According to Einstein's theory of special relativity, the faster an object goes (most noticeably, as it approaches the speed of light) the more, to an outside observer, it slows down in time. If and when that object hits the speed of light, time stops completely—the object can grow no older. We all hurtle through the space-time continuum, but when we divert all possible velocity into movement through space none is left over for temporal change. Our time simply comes to a halt.

In the words of Brian Greene, physicist-author of *The Elegant Universe*, "Thus light does not get old: a photon that emerged from the big bang is the same age today as it was then. There is no passage of time at light speed." We can observe these photons, now stretched out to the length of microwaves, bathing the entirety of the universe.

Through the ages philosophers and theologians have searched for an eternal in the immaterial realm—the ideal Form, the disembodied God—yet the eternal surrounds us right here. Flip on a light switch and there it is—your room is filled with particles destined for immortality. They will be here billions of years after that light bulb (and your and my body) has burned out. And marvelously, they will not age one whit over these millennia but still cavort like fresh-born babies. Time without end, amen.

Only thus do we sense the full meaning of "And God said, 'Let there be light.'" In light, eternity plunged into time, and yet retained its eternal form. At the heart of change we find the unchanging. At the speed of light—the swiftest of all motions—we find what is ever still. Realize this and become *enlightened*.

Today, turn on a light switch and witness a miracle. Realize the eternal nature of these dancing photons.

The Dark Universe
The Glory of All We Don't Know

❖

I do not know what I may appear to the world; but to myself I seem to have been only like a boy playing on the sea-shore, and diverting myself in now and then finding a smoother pebble or a prettier shell than ordinary, whilst the great ocean of truth lay all undiscovered before me.

ISAAC NEWTON,
BREWSTER'S MEMOIRS OF NEWTON

❖

At the time I write this I can state with absolute certainty that most of the universe is missing. It used to be thought the universe was mainly made of stars and galaxies—the kind of stuff you see shining down at night. But then we realized that this "normal" matter constituted but a fraction of the universe's contents—about four percent by current estimates. What is the rest, and where is it? We can infer by a variety of effects that a much greater proportion of the universe is constituted out of "dark matter." The "dark" refers to the fact that it is not luminous like the stars, nor does it radiate other forms of detectable energy—in fact, we simply *can't find it anywhere*. Dark matter might be made out of conventional stuff, cosmic dust grains, rocks, and the like—or high velocity subatomic particles like neutrinos ("hot dark matter") or low-velocity particles ("cold dark matter"), or possibly a combination of all.

To make matters worse, it has recently been discovered that even more significant is "dark energy." Something is exerting a repulsive force (a kind of "negative gravity") that is accelerating the expansion of our universe. But we can't find this energy either, and don't have a great theory (another way to say this is we have *too many theories*) for what it might be. If dark matter makes up close to a quarter of the universe, dark energy seems to account for most of the other three-quarters. We simply don't know where or what most of our universe is. Careless to have misplaced something so large.

Scientists will search for it and no doubt do some finding. But it seems to be a perpetual truth that the more we know the more we realize what we don't know (or how little we know). We explode our horizons outward and discover that what we thought was the All, is just the tiniest fragment. As recently as the 1920s it was believed that the Milky Way was the entirety of the universe. Now we realize it is but $1/100,000,000,000$ of the visible galactic universe, and that in turn may be but the tiniest part of the totality of all that originated in the Big Bang. Even the Big Bang may be but one in a possibly infinite series of universe-creations. We finally exceed the limits of what *can* be known.

This is good to remember when we grow too enamored of our intellect. It can look like we stride the earth like gods. We seem all-knowing, and hence all-powerful, in our rule. Thankfully our minds—the source of this power—also expose to us our limitations. We realize this earth we seem to rule over is but a molecule in a mote of dust resting on a grain of sand on one of the innumerable beaches of a boundless ocean. Socrates was right: True knowledge is knowing how much you don't know. We need not only the Theologians to help us walk humbly but the Scientists as well. Despite their warfare over the centuries both groups can here find common ground: We dwell in darkness upon darkness, forever doomed to say "Huh?"

Today, stop to ponder for a moment how much you, even we as a species, do not know. Don't view this as a negative but as a revelation of the mystery and majesty of the Whole.

Quantum Mechanics
The Creativity of Chance

"God does not play dice." So goes Einstein's famous response to the then novel science of quantum mechanics. Now a widely accepted discipline, capable of astoundingly accurate predictions concerning the subatomic world, quantum mechanics introduced to physics an element of chance.

LaPlace, working within a classical framework, stated that if you knew the initial conditions of the world, the distribution of matter and energy, given the deterministic nature of physical laws you could foretell every event across future millennia. No word uttered, no baby born, no leaf blown hither and yon, would fail to be predictable in its minutest detail. In a sense, there'd be nothing new under the sun, or anywhere in the universe, the sun itself included.

But classical physics suffers radical breakdown on the subatomic level. Here's where quantum mechanics has proven its theoretical and experimental power. Its framework is not deterministic but probabilistic. Describing a light source emitting billions of photons it can predict with great accuracy how many will end up where. But whether a single photon aimed between two diffraction slits will pass through the left or the right cannot be predicted. It's a fifty-fifty proposition. Where it will go is unpredictable *in theory*, not only in practice, given the wave-particle duality of quantum events and the Heisenberg uncertainty principle. This is not a limitation based on the design of our equipment, but built insurmountably into the structure of the universe. And this quantum unpredictability has very real effects. Even in a vacuum seemingly devoid of matter and energy, through quantum chance particles and anti-particles flash into existence, usually to annihilate one another and disappear almost instantaneously. Yet this churning virtual soup presides over a strange appearance of energy and matter, something out of nothing, continuously.

It is now hypothesized by leading physicists that this is the very source of our universe. It may have derived from the chance precipitation of energy/matter out of the quantum void, which then exploded outward in the Big Bang. If so, as physicist Alan Guth writes, the universe is the "ultimate free lunch." We may then have to reverse Einstein's perspective: Perhaps God *does* play dice with the universe. Maybe the universe itself originated from a roll of quantum dice.

Not just a shock to the world of science, this may seem religious heresy. We are used to thinking of God as a ruler whose long arm dictates every action within his kingdom. Divine law, political law, scientific law, all intertwine around the notion of a universe well regulated and controlled.

But wouldn't it be interesting if God *did* play with dice? Imagine a board game where, given initial conditions and the rules of the game, every subsequent move is predictable. Boring. Little point in playing. The game's over at the start. In many human games we add some dice, a spinner, a shuffled deck, or another way to insert the unpredictable. We invite chance, the great trickster, to play. He scrambles game patterns, invents novel twists, surprises and challenges the talents of the players.

Who is to say God (Creative Energy) doesn't operate this way? Physicists speak of the probabilistic world of quantum mechanics. Biologists tell us that the random mutations of genes are key to the evolution of species. They keep stirring the biotic stew, giving rise to new flavors.

And in a human life, chance, as much as design, is the engine of our breakthroughs and soul-growth. Face it: The game of life, the game of the universe, may come equipped with a pair of dice.

Think for a moment about how some chance occurrences and meetings have dramatically altered your life. Must you resist this notion, or can you embrace it as part of the game?

Wormholes
Passage to Another World

Scientists have theorized about so-called "wormholes" in our universe. Formed from a black hole, now collapsed into a "singularity" of no radius and infinite density, this "wormhole" might allow matter to flow right through it into an alternate region or universe. It thus would serve as a sort of secret passageway, a tunnel from one reality into another. Science fiction writers love the stuff. It opens up a journey between worlds.

Children's books are also filled with wormholes. When Alice plunges into the white rabbit's hole she emerges in another universe run by its own bizarre rules. So, too, when Gulliver lands on the island of the Lilliputians, when Mary Lennox of *The Secret Garden* stumbles upon this special place, or when Dorothy is tossed into Oz by a twister. It is no surprise that children's literature is filled with wormholes, because so are children, with their vibrant imaginations. A child can enter alternate universes at the drop of a hat, the wormhole-hat of that mad hatter called fantasy.

It is not only the child's world that is filled with wormholes but that of the spiritual seeker. In meditation you may focus on a point just below the navel and follow the breath in and out of there for days, months, or years. Pointless? No, there is a point, a one-pointed focus, that can finally turn into a wormhole. It transports you from a frantic, scattered relation to reality into that place where all becomes One.

For Christians, the Eucharist can form such a wormhole. Alice had to swallow a magical cake to be able to fit down the rabbit hole. So, too, a nibble of Christ's body and blood can open a passageway to God.

Then, too, many religious work with a mantra, a repetitive prayer. The Christian may repeat the name of Jesus, or the Hindu that of Ram. The Buddhist might use "Om mani padme hum" (meaning "the All is a jewel in the lotus of the heart"). Over time, the mantra opens a tunnel home.

Then there are alluring but false wormholes. Booze, heroin, gambling—these may simulate passage to a better world filled with expansive sensation or ease. Yet they can prove a shortcut to nowhere.

Then there are wormholes that suck us in by surprise. We are listening to a Bach cantata, or wandering in a forest, when suddenly we feel part of a different world—more clear, gathered, alive. All is okay, or if it's not okay, that's okay. Our awareness seems emptier, yet thereby more full. We abide there for a while until we are spit back out into the ordinary.

But we don't fully forget. And so we meditate on the navel, or chant, or pray, or do whatever might open that wormhole.

When in your life have you entered a wormhole to the spiritual realm? What practices or experiences seem to open this up for you?

The Big Bang

How Once We Were One

*N*ot everybody agrees on everything in modern-day cosmology. In fact, there are a multitude of questions left unanswered about the processes that built our universe and will determine its future. But most people in the field agree on this: Our universe began some 13.7 billion years ago in a "Big Bang." From a "singularity," a point of infinite density and space-time curvature (from which sprang space, time, and the physical laws of our cosmos) the universe began. It exploded outward into a sea of quarks, then forming protons and neutrons, and then the nuclei of helium, lithium, and deuterium, which later gave rise to neutral atoms then forming clouds of gas that congealed into stars and galaxies, finally giving rise to beings like ourselves.

We might say that in a sense we *remember* the Big Bang. After all, it is imprinted on our bodies. The elementary particles that make us up were created in the Big Bang. Their synthesis into atoms came later—primarily in the furnace of burning stars—but we can trace our material substance back to the first second of the universe. In this sense, we are very *old beings*, as is everything in our universe.

We may not consciously recollect this event, but something in us longs to *re-collect:* to re-gather our dispersed universe back into that singularity. The mystical sense that we are one with the cosmos may be a trace "memory" of our origin. We really were one then—not just spiritually but materially. Or perhaps we cannot even contrast spirit and matter: The Big Bang is prior to all such distinctions.

That the universe exploded apart is a good thing. But it was also a loss, a shattering of Self that we subconsciously long to heal. When we fall in love, or care for an ill person, or gaze in wonder at the stars, aren't these strategies of re-union? We are, every one of us, Big Bang alumni, members of the class of '00 heading toward our fourteenth reunion (14 billion years, that is). Why miss the fun of coming back to the One?

What are the ways in which the longing to be One, within yourself, with others, and with the natural world, manifests itself in your life? Are you making time in such ways to "go to your reunion"?

SHAPE-SHIFT
Pretend You Are at the Big Bang

BENEFITS: experiencing your Divine Self and the energies underlying the universe.

Find a comfortable and stable position in which to sit. You are about to re-create, over and over, a universe. On the in-breath pull the air into a single point located in your chest or your abdomen. Feel all the energies condense right there, as if it were a singularity without dimension. Then, on the out-breath, let this single point explode outward into a universe. Imagine your out-breath as a Big Bang producing stars and planets, galaxies, even space and time itself. Follow the out-breath beyond the limits of your body, feeling yourself as the universe expanding.

On the next in-breath feel this universe contract back to a single point within your body. You may pause a moment and feel the stoppage of time. (There is no time until produced by the next Big Bang.) Repeat this cycle of contraction and expansion for however many breaths you wish. This is a highly energetic meditation so you may not wish to sustain it as long as some others.

Note: On the in-breath you might say to yourself "I." On the out-breath say "Am." Combine this "I Am" mantra with the visualization above. When Moses asks God his name, he replies "I am that I am." Gathering the breath into a single point, we experience the unity of the cosmic "I." Exploding outward we experience the "Am" of God's Being creating a universe.

epilogue

Tips for Spark-Hunters

*T*ogether we have uncovered sparks of the divine. Perhaps you, the reader, have found some enjoyment, edification, or inspiration in the one hundred pieces here assembled. Perhaps some left you bored or perplexed. No matter. Far more important than any of the essays is the example they set of an ongoing practice: that of unearthing sacred sparks.

To incorporate this into daily life is, according to Kabbalah, to hallow our world. At the same time we hallow our own life. We find a constant fount of joy and meaning in our interactions with others. By others I mean not only other people but the glorious landscapes and creatures of nature and the objects of the human world amidst which we dwell. The blue jay in our backyard; the car we drive to work; the windswept beach we visit in the summer; our toilet bowl with its cleansing flush; God is hidden everywhere if we but know how to look.

That brings us to the closing, and most important, question of the book—how to uncover these sparks. The first answer that occurs to me: *I don't know.* Revelation always retains its mystery, its flavor of unmerited grace. (The essays in this book were mostly just "given to me," guided by sudden experience and an inner voice that I took down like dictation.) Second answer, equally dismaying: *We can't.* We can't just wrench sparks out of the world by willpower any more than a sailboat can motor to shore. It must await the merciful wind.

Yet the wind will do no good unless a sail be at the ready to catch it. This leads to a third, more hopeful answer to the question of how to find divine sparks: *We can engage in practices of attentiveness and receptivity.* We can expect such sparks, come to look for them, and stand still long enough to receive their gifts. (I, myself, a restless, inattentive intellectual, am far from a natural spark-finder, but I am trying to learn more the art.) Let me propose five such practices that may help us with our spark-finding.

1. Pay Attention

Let's take it for granted (disagree if you wish) that we go through much of life distracted, preoccupied, and constricted by the stuff of our all-too-busy lives, and even more so, our all-too-busy minds. To get out of our mental prison, to pay attention to the outer world, proves no easy task. But it can be a fun and fulfilling one, especially if we engage the art playfully. Here then are some "games" of attention.

"How many things can I notice?" In this game (I like to play it when I go out for a walk), see how many new things you can notice. I like to set a goal—I will find at least *ten* things or *twenty.* Walking down a tree-lined street in my neighborhood I see the play of light and shadow on the leaves; I notice the slightly brighter shade of green of the bush tips signaling their growing edge; I hear three different bird-calls, no, four—no, five—hovering in the air above. Soon the world reveals itself as a luminous place, playing forth like a symphony.

"Bless you!" Proceed through your day as if it were filled with blessings. Sinking into a hot bath, luxuriate in its liquidy caress. Say to the bath, "Bless you," or realize it is saying "Bless you" to you in its own watery fashion. Time to brush your teeth—savor the blessings of fresh breath and a clean smile. A sip of coffee—bless that surge of energy that will make the day seem possible.

"For the first time." In this game, encounter an object as if for the very first time. Pretend you are an alien from outer space, or

a young and very sheltered child, or a person who grew up in a faraway place. For whatever reason, this is the very first time you have ever seen a grape—or a flower—or whatever you want to play with. Pretend you don't even know the names of the objects, or their familiar uses. See them, touch them, taste them, with your senses fully engaged. Strange wonders will be revealed.

"How slow can I go?" In this game (easily combined with the others) linger lovingly over an object or activity for as long as you can. Eat a cookie, but take five minutes to do it so you savor every aspect of its being. Or seeing a squirrel outside your window, spend the time to track it through sight and sound. Notice the agility and humor of its movement, the softness of its fur contrasted with sharp claws, its habits and preferences, and on and on. Paying attention is not so much about "doing something" as a not-doing-something that enables us to simply *be* and *receive*.

2. Worship Beauty

Paying attention leads to an associated principle—worship beauty wherever you can. This may sound like a "mom and apple pie" principle—who doesn't like beauty and want more of it in their lives? But increasingly the contemplation of beauty has been reduced to a marginal luxury (too much to do!) and understood in purely aesthetic terms. "Pretty as a picture," we say, contemplating a sunset. Yes, but that's the problem. The scene looks like a postcard or the background to our bank checks. To see the world in this pre-digested and commodified way is truly *not to see it:* The sunset is no longer luminous.

How different to *worship* beauty; to stand in awe of what surrounds us; to sense the divine fire that shines forth in things. Let us regard the search for and appreciation of such encounters as a central spiritual practice.

So seek out the environments that most move you with their beauty. That may be the beach with its lulling waves, its soothing sand, its never-ending horizons. Or maybe you love the cool green of the forest, or a mountaintop's windy vistas. Go there. Make time. Make the trip. You will hold these images in your heart for years to come.

Then too, there are probably scenes of beauty closer to home and more easily available. An early morning walk before the world has awoken; the city park with twittering birds that actually drown out the honking taxis; that single flower resting in a vase on your desk—gather up what bits of beauty you can find. Turn on some lovely music when it's time to pay the bills. Cover that crack in the wall with the earth-toned quilt sitting unused up in the attic. Insist on beauty not as luxury, but necessity for your soul.

3. Listen for Lessons

Uncovering sparks is not only about finding beauty but also learning lessons on how to live. We have seen in the one hundred essays of the book how the objects that surround us can become our teachers if we have the willingness to sign on as pupils.

Perhaps that sounds unappetizing, especially if you hated schools and teachers. Again, it can work well to make a game of it. Wherever you are—say you're in your kitchen—look around—choose even an unlikely suspect—for example, your toaster. Now imagine that toaster is your spiritual guide with something crucial to teach. What might it be? Free associate, enlisting your mind, your humor, your subconscious, and the revelatory power of God. Hmmm. A toaster must be placed on the right setting to cook a piece of bread properly. Hold onto the bread too long and it will burn. Is there a relationship, a project, in your life that you're holding onto even at the risk of ruining it? Maybe it's time to let go, to let it pop out before it turns crisp and blackened.

Then too, a toaster only works properly when connected to its power source. You may, on occasion, have waited and waited for your bagel (I have!) only to realize the darn toaster wasn't plugged in. Is there an area in your life you feel stalled? Maybe the toaster is reminding you to plug into your Higher Power, seeking the needed energy and guidance.

In addition to playfully asking advice of random objects, seek out your special guides. A Native American tribe often has a single totem animal that operates as spirit guide and protector. Be it wolf, bear, or eagle, the power embodied in this creature, its cunning, wisdom, strength, and abilities, are accessed for special help.

Ask yourself, what is *your* totem animal? The hawk that flies high above the world, or your cat who teaches you, on a daily basis, how to curl and purr? Let your intuition guide you to your guide. And what is your totem plant? The persistent climbing ivy; the crocus so eager for spring? Plant it in your garden, but ever more so, plant it in your heart and listen for its special teachings. Finally, what is your totem object or objects drawn from the human-made world? Your toaster? The gentle fan that cools you when overheated? The sofa downstairs that reminds you to relax?

Perhaps the one hundred essays of this book can help you locate such guides. Ask yourself which pieces particularly resonated with you. Stay with those messages, objects, and beings for they may have more to teach. But don't hesitate to go beyond my words and themes. I described some of my special teachers but yours may be entirely different.

Speak with your guides as you might a spiritual director or a friend. Or if you wish, write essays or journal entries, perhaps a bit like those you have found in this book. Let your writing arise from close attention to the object and to an inward voice. (I like to engage in a sort of automatic writing where things pour forth—from God?—from my subconscious?—as I sit at the computer.)

With time you may be done with particular guides and feel ready to seek out new ones. They may shift from day to day, even moment to moment. But assume you will never be bereft: that you are ever surrounded by object-lessons and creature-teachers and that God will use them well.

4. Shape-Shift

It is good to consult with creature-teachers; it can be better yet to *turn into them* and absorb their wisdom from within. A shaman doesn't just speak with a spirit-animal but magically or imaginatively becomes it. I think that we all have an archaic urge—bodily, mentally, spiritually—to explore our more-than-human identity by "shape-shifting." The meditations supplied in the book provide some opportunities. You may wish to continue using one or more, or make up your own. Assume that you have the ability in meditation to experience from within that landscape, animal, plant, or object for which you have a special affinity. Use your imaginative capacities to take off your skin and try on that of another being.

You may also wish to explore any of the shape-shifting "technologies" that have been gifted to us from diverse cultures. Do yoga and really get into the "cobra" pose or "dog" pose, or "tree." Explore Chinese Qigong (Chi Kung), Tai Chi, or any of a variety of martial arts where you balance earthly and heavenly energies, learning to flow like water and move like the wind. You may find you not only dwell in the universe, but that the whole universe dwells within you.

5. Cultivate the Spirit

A final recommendation for aspiring spark-hunters: Cultivate your spiritual practices. Which ones? Whichever ones work for you. Maybe you are a meditator. You enjoy sinking into the inward silence. Maybe you have a devotional spirit and love the rituals of worship, the intimacy of prayer. Maybe you are cerebral and find that a good book of metaphysics—or astrophysics— shakes your tree. Maybe you'd rather be *doing something for someone.* You feel God's presence through active service.

Whichever your path, walk it with fervor. You will likely find (I have) that whatever opens you up spiritually—however distant it seems from the specific practices I've been discussing—helps open you to sparks of the divine. Our sight is cleansed, our world illuminated, when we're on our way back home.

Of course this journey also leads us right back to where we started, immersed in our ordinary life. Everything is as it was: There's still laundry to do, the garbage to take out. Yet we may find that everything also looks quite different when lit up by sparks of the divine. As Martin Buber writes in *The Way of Man According to the Teaching of Hasidism:*

It is said of a certain Talmudic master that the paths of heaven were as bright to him as the streets of his native town. Hasidism inverts the order: It is a greater thing if the streets of a man's native town are as bright to him as the paths of heaven. For it is here, where we stand, that we should try to make shine the light of the hidden divine life.

Amen.

Acknowledgments

Working on this book was a more solitary experience than any of my previous efforts. I mainly wrote alone, and in shyness kept the results to myself for a good long time. Yet, this solitude was anything but isolating. The experiences recorded in this book are those of *communion*—with the ravishing landscapes of nature; the gentle lessons of household things; and, most of all, with the voice of God within. Though never was a book of mine more conceived in solitude, never have I felt less ownership of it, for the ideas and words came as gift.

On the human level, I have likewise been the blessed receiver. I thank Beth Kingsley Hawkins for her stunning photographs, which spring the book to visual life. Others have taught to me to love the natural world and human body. David Strong, hiker and chronicler of the Crazy Mountains, comes to mind, and David Abram, an ecological magician. Nancy Romita, skilled teacher of the Alexander Technique, showed me how to transform the body into sand or give it a good steam cleaning. Jon Kabat-Zinn meditates on the self as mountain or lake, another source of the book's shape-shifting. Rabbi Zalman Schachter-Shalomi and Aryeh Lev Stollman helped with Kabbalah, and Father Frank Haig with the Kabbalah of contemporary astrophysics.

On matters literary, I am indebted to Shelley Roth, my ever supportive agent who kept the spark alive; Bob Wicks who helped transmit it to Sorin Books, where it was fanned by Bob Hamma and Karen Shannon, who have proved such a pleasure to work with.

In the background, Loyola College in Maryland—its philoso-phy department, faculty, and administration—have provided unfailing support for my unorthodox work. Their granted sabbatical leave gave me the needed time to write.

Then too, nothing happens without help on the home front. I give my love and gratitude to Janice McLane, and my children, Anna-Rose and Sarah, for the light that burns so bright in the hearth of our hearts.

Dr. Drew Leder has blended an unusual array of interests and accomplishments. He has an M.D. from Yale University School of Medicine, and a Ph.D. in philosophy from the State University of New York at Stony Brook. He is currently a full professor of Western and Eastern Philosophy at Loyola College in Maryland.

Dr. Leder is the author of several books, including *Games for the Soul: 40 Playful Ways to Find Fun and Fulfillment in a Stressful World* (Hyperion, 1998). Another book, *Spiritual Passages: Embracing Life's Sacred Journey* (Tarcher/Putnam, 1997), grew out of work Dr. Leder did on cross-cultural views of aging, begun as a Scholar-in-Residence at Chicago's prestigious Park Ridge Center. Dr. Leder continues to offer lectures and workshops on spirituality and aging, and acts as a consultant to educational and residential communities with this interest.

Dr. Leder's earlier, more academic writing focused on bodily experience in health and illness. He is the author of *The Absent Body* (U. of Chicago Press, 1990), editor of *The Body in Medical Thought and Practice* (Kluwer, 1992), and assistant editor of the *Encyclopedia of Bioethics* (Macmillan, 1995).

In addition, Dr. Leder has worked extensively with prisoners in a maximum security environment. Using philosophical and spiritual tools, he has explored with them the nature of violence, incarceration, and self-transformation. The result of this work has appeared in different magazines, and is the subject of his new book, *The Soul Knows No Bars: Inmates Reflect on Life, Death, and Hope* (preface by Cornel West; Rowman and Littlefield, 2000).

Dr. Leder's work has garnered a good deal of media attention. Articles by or about him have appeared in such places as *Family Circle*, *The Washington Post*, *Chicago Tribune*, *Baltimore Sun*, and other magazines and newspapers around the country. He has appeared extensively on national and local TV and radio.

Dr. Leder has also spoken at conferences around the country, and participated in panels, workshops, and think-tanks in a variety of settings, including the Omega Institute and Esalen, along with more traditional scholarly forums. He is committed to reaching as wide an audience as possible through his books, articles, workshops, retreats, and audio tapes.

Immersed In the Sacred
Discovering the "Small s" Sacraments
Kathy Coffey
ISBN: 0-87793-962-4 / $12.95
Every place can be a doorway to the sacred and every activity can be a vehicle for grace. Kathy Coffey invites us to reflect and find the holy in the people, places, activities, and objects that fill our lives.

Savoring God
Praying With All Our Senses
Kathleen Finley
ISBN: 0-87793-981-0 / $12.95
Enliven your prayer life by changing your focus. In **Savoring God**, Kathleen Finley shows how to find God in everyday objects by taking another look, listen, taste, touch, and smell. Includes prayer, mediation, scripture, reflection, and guidance for action.

Tickle Your Soul
Live Well, Love Much, Laugh Often
Anne Bryan Smollin
ISBN: 1-893732-00-2 / $12.95
Enables readers to "wrinkle their faces with smiles" and avoid "drying up their souls like prunes."
Tickle Your Soul delivers joy, health, and wellness.

In Pursuit of the Great White Rabbit
Edward Hays
ISBN: 0-939516-13-6 / $11.95
The Mystical White Rabbit, whom we usually call God, must be chased like hounds in eager pursuit. Parables, practical advice, and spiritual insights for finding God in the commonplace corners of life.

Secular Sanctity
Edward Hays
ISBN: 0-939516-05-5 / $10.95
This wise and practical handbook for seeking the sacred in the secular world offers you 18 challenging essays on finding holiness in such everyday areas of life as organic reading, hospitality, sexual spirituality, music, letter writing, work, sacred idleness, and meditation.

Prices and availability subject to change. Available at your local bookstore, online retailers, and from Ave Maria Press at **www.avemariapress.com** or **1-800-282-1865**

KEYCODE: FØTØ1Ø4ØØØØ